FROM BURMA TO MYANMAR

On the Road to Mandalay

LYDIA LAUBE

Wakefield Press

Wakefield Press
16 Rose Street
Mile End
South Australia 5031
www.wakefieldpress.com.au

First published 2015

Cover designed by Dean Lahn, Lahn Stafford Design
Typeset by Wakefield Press
Printed in Australia by Griffin Digital, Adelaide

National Library of Australia Cataloguing-in-Publication entry

Creator:	Laube, Lydia, 1948– , author.
Title:	From Burma to Myanmar: on the road to Mandalay / Lydia Laube.
ISBN:	978 1 74305 392 8 (paperback).
Subjects:	Laube, Lydia, 1948– , – Travel. Myanmar – Description and travel. Mandalay (Burma) – Description and travel.
Dewey Number:	910.4

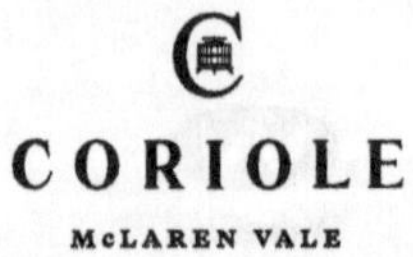

Wakefield Press

FROM BURMA TO MYANMAR

Lydia Laube never says no to adventure, whether that means galloping a horse across the Mongolian plains or hopping on a cargo ship to Madagascar. Born into the farming community of Caltowie in the mid-north of South Australia, Lydia trained as a nurse in Adelaide, then set off to see the world. Her debut book, *Behind the Veil: An Australian nurse in Saudi Arabia*, was an instant bestseller, and she has become one of Australia's favourite travel writers. *From Burma to Myanmar* is Lydia's ninth travel yarn.

Between winter escapes to the sun, Lydia Laube shares a small house in Adelaide with a large cat with attitude.

Also by Lydia Laube

Behind the Veil

Bound for Vietnam

Is this the Way to Madagascar?

Llama for Lunch

Lost in Laos

Slow Boat to Mongolia

Temples and Tuk Tuks

The Long Way Home

Contents

Mandalay

Rudyard Kipling

By the old Moulmein Pagoda, lookin' eastward to the sea,
There's a Burma girl a-settin', and I know she thinks o' me;
For the wind is in the palm-trees, and the temple-bells they say:
'Come you back, you British soldier; come you back to Mandalay!'
Come you back to Mandalay,
Where the old Flotilla lay:
Can't you 'ear their paddles clunkin' from Rangoon to Mandalay?
On the road to Mandalay,
Where the flyin'-fishes play,
An' the dawn comes up like thunder outer China 'crost the Bay!

'Er petticoat was yaller an' 'er little cap was green,
An' 'er name was Supi-yaw-lat – jes' the same as Theebaw's Queen,
An' I seed her first a-smoking of a whackin' white cheroot,
An' a-wastin' Christian kisses on an 'eathen idol's foot:
Bloomin' idol made o' mud –
Wot they called the Great Gawd Budd –
Plucky lot she cared for idols when I kissed 'er where she stud!
On the road to Mandalay …

When the mist was on the rice-fields an' the sun was droppin' slow,
She'd git 'er little banjo an' she'd sing 'Kulla-lo-lo'
With 'er arm upon my shoulder an' 'er check agin' my cheek
We useter watch the steamers an' the hathis pilin' teak.
Elephints a-pilin' teak
In the sludgy, squdgy creek,
Where the silence 'ung that 'eavy you was 'arf afraid to speak!
On the road to Mandalay …

But that's all shove be'ind me – long ago an' fur away,
An' there ain't no 'busses runnin' from the Bank to Mandalay;
An' I'm learnin' 'ere in London what the ten-year soldier tells:
'If you've 'eard the East a-callin', you won't never 'eed naught else.'
No! you won't 'eed nothin' else
But them spicy garlic smells,
An' the sunshine an' the palm-trees an' the tinkly temple-bells;
On the road to Mandalay …

I am sick o' wastin' leather on these gritty pavin'-stones,
An' the blasted English drizzle wakes the fever in my bones;
Tho' I walks with fifty 'ousemaids outer Chelsea to the Strand,
An' they talks a lot o' lovin', but wot do they understand?
Beefy face an' grubby 'and –
Law! wot do they understand?
I've a neater, sweeter maiden in a cleaner, greener land!
On the road to Mandalay …

Ship me somewheres east of Suez, where the best is like the worst,
Where there aren't no Ten Commandments an' a man can raise a thirst;
For the temple-bells are callin', an' it's there that I would be –
By the old Moulmein Pagoda, looking lazy at the sea;
On the road to Mandalay,
Where the old Flotilla lay,
With our sick beneath the awnings when we went to Mandalay!
On the road to Mandalay,
Where the flyin'-fishes play,
An' the dawn comes up like thunder outer China 'crost the Bay!

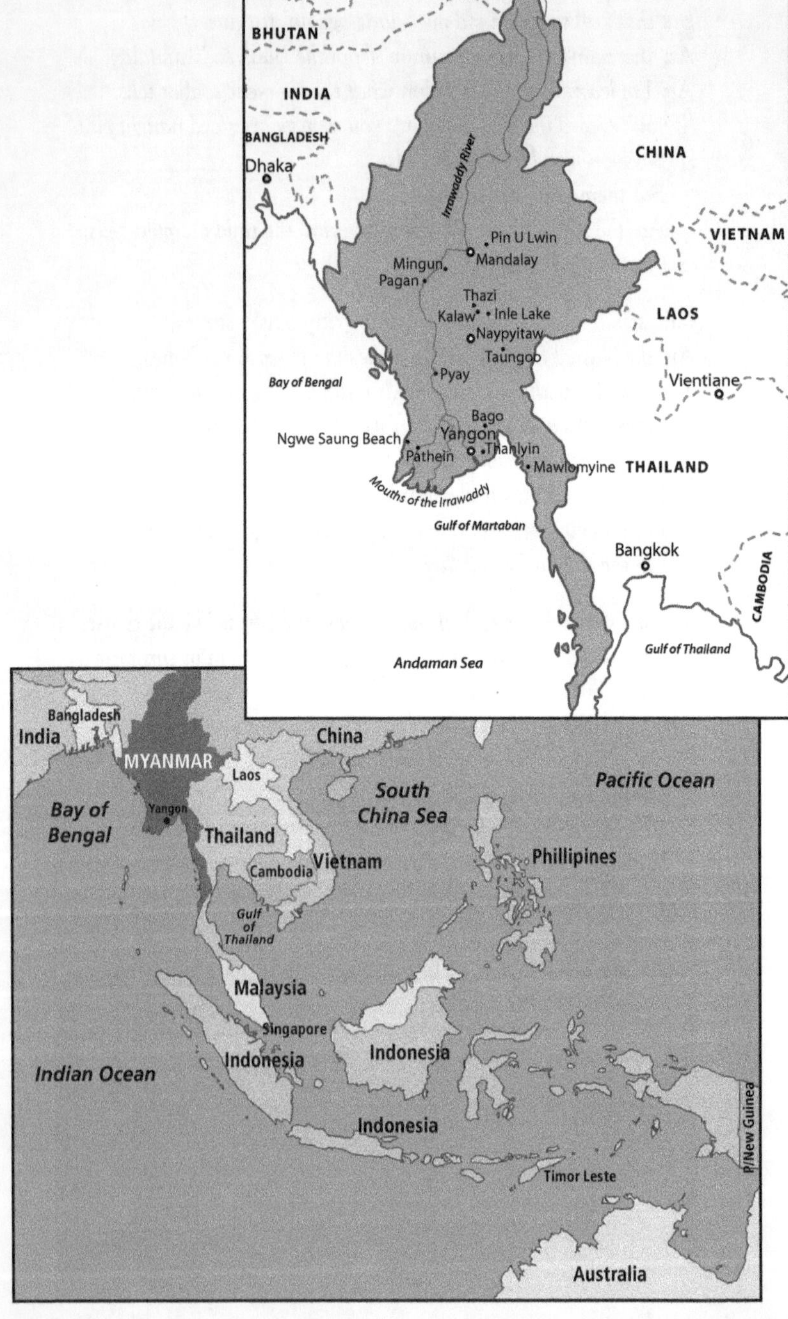
BHUTAN
INDIA
BANGLADESH
Dhaka
CHINA
Irrawaddy River
VIETNAM
Pin U Lwin
Mandalay
Mingun
Pagan
Thazi
Kalaw
Inle Lake
LAOS
Naypyitaw
Taungoo
Pyay
Bay of Bengal
Vientiane
Bago
Yangon
Ngwe Saung Beach
Pathein
Thanlyin
Mawlomyine
THAILAND
Mouths of the Irrawaddy
Gulf of Martaban
Bangkok
CAMBODIA
Gulf of Thailand
Andaman Sea
Bangladesh
India
MYANMAR
China
Laos
Pacific Ocean
Bay of Bengal
Yangon
South China Sea
Thailand
Phillipines
Cambodia
Vietnam
Gulf of Thailand
Malaysia
Singapore
Indonesia
Indonesia
Indian Ocean
Indonesia
P/New Guinea
Timor Leste
Australia

chapter **1**

'Last night I dreamt I went to Manderley again.'
Famous first line of Daphne du Maurier's book, *Rebecca.*

I, too, dreamed of going back to Mandalay, but it was Burma's Mandalay, not Daphne's 'Manderley' I dreamed of.

So why was I now on my way back to Burma for the fifth time? It wasn't even Burma any more. Now it was Myanmar. Still, something about this country attracted me – unfinished business maybe. Or the appeal of the forbidden. Burma has in the past been enticingly coy about letting me in.

The first time I travelled to Burma, over twenty years ago, I was accompanied by my sister. We zoomed around the country at the speed of light. There was no time to stop and smell the flowers as tourists were allowed to stay only one week – an improvement, however, on the twenty-four hours permitted after General Ne Win's 1962 coup. The government he established – the world's longest running military dictatorship – installed an isolationist policy that virtually closed the country to outsiders.

They might have kicked you out after a week but the powers that ruled Burma with an iron, if incomprehensible, fist didn't mind how many times you flew in and out. That first brief visit had been enough to show us that Burma was a beautiful country of charming people so we decided to fly out and return again almost immediately.

We started from Bangkok, the best and closest place to

get a Burmese visa. Arriving on a stopover deal with Thai International, we spent two nights at the wonderful Royal Orchid Hotel on the riverfront of the Chao Phraya River in central Bangkok, indulging in sumptuous breakfasts and, between bursts of temples and markets, watching the busy river traffic from our tenth-floor room.

Then, visa in hand, we flew on to Rangoon with Thai International, the only permitted way to enter Burma. All other points were and still are off-limits, even though Burma shares borders with India, China, Bangladesh, Laos and Thailand and has an 1199-mile coastline on the Bay of Bengal and the Andaman Sea.

Immediately on arrival we began to play the universal game of Beat the Government Currency Racket. Burmese money was tightly controlled and tourists were supposed to use the much-inflated government rates of the kyat, which you had to buy with US dollars. All exchanges and purchases had to be recorded on a form that was checked when you left the country to prove you had used government sanctioned cash. The only hotels allowed to accept tourists were government owned and their bills had to be paid in dollars. This draconian system presented a challenge not to be ignored by those of us who did not want to give our money to a less than nice government. We fiddled the forms to make it look as though we had changed more money than we had, and paid wherever possible with kyat, which we obtained on the black market, a thriving industry that gave you ten times the official rate. Sometimes we were able to stay (illegally) at small hotels who allowed us (illegally) to pay in kyats that we had obtained (illegally again) on the black market. Another lurk travellers used to obtain a wad of unofficial kyat was to buy bottles of Black Label Johnny Walker whisky and cartons of American cigarettes – both prized and unobtainable in Burma – in the duty free shop and then sell them to one of the buyers waiting immediately outside the airport terminal. We did this and it provided a handsome profit in a wad of local money. We were off to a grand start in our life of crime. I found the wheeling and dealing and intrigue to outwit the government great fun, and I was very successful at it too. Did you know that 10 can easily be made into 100 if you find a black pen that looks the same as the one used to record your original amount exchanged?

Black market dealers were everywhere. The most reliable were the taxi drivers who hung about outside the Grand Hotel in Rangoon. They would either drive you around the corner to make the deal or take you to someone who would. We dealt whenever possible with the same man we came to trust. We learnt very quickly that only the government cheated you in Burma.

The Grand was where we spent our first night. It sat facing the Yangon River on Strand Road among a row of other once impressive colonial piles. Formerly wonderful but now faded and shabby, a double room in this old British hotel cost ten dollars. Now, since the government has tarted it up, you can hardly get a drink there for that, and rooms start at around four hundred.

Faded or not, I loved The Grand's ambience. Entering the hotel from the street, climbing its unswept grimy steps, we found ourselves in a foyer redolent of the Raj, dominated by a great polished wooden bar surrounded by old leather armchairs. Our ballroom-sized room came with an enormous bathroom containing ancient fixtures, a cavernous bath and understandably faulty plumbing.

It would be a dash to get in and out of Burma – a fairly large country, a bit bigger than France – in one week, so we left Rangoon the next night on the train to Mandalay.

Burma has never had a quiet life. For hundreds of years, until 1885 when Britain took control, it contained many small warring kingdoms. Rebellion was still rife among ethnic minority groups and Karen insurgents would demonstrate their displeasure with the government by coming down from the hills every now and then to blow up the Mandalay train. While I sympathised with their grudge against the government, I didn't want to be sent heavenwards by one of their bombs. I spent the night anticipating a loud bang and clung tightly to my top bunk, not only because it was a very rocky ride. The explosion failed to materialise and we arrived safely in Mandalay the next morning.

Mandalay was all I had expected. With its old royal palace and mountain-top temples, it felt far more Burmese than Rangoon had. We climbed the hundreds of steps that led up to the temple on the top of Mandalay Hill, in order to achieve good karma as well as to look down on the town from a great height.

After two days we found a share taxi and travelled up into the mountains north-east of Mandalay to Maymyo (now Pyin Oo Lwin), a former hill station of the British. Parts of Burma are mountainous; further north the Kachin Hills lead into the Himalayas. Up there in Maymyo, among pine forests and green hills that climb to the Shan Plateau, it was wonderfully cool after the heat of the plains. We stayed in another place you'd not get into today, the Candacraig Hotel. Surrounded by large trees and green lawns, it looked like a wooden chalet transposed from somewhere in Europe. At night we sat in front of open log fires drinking hot mandarin juice laced with local gin and by day we rode around in quaint horse-drawn buggies.

After this delightful interlude it was back by train for another night at the Strand and a taxi to the airport. Our driver had a few mishaps on the way and we just managed to make it onto the end of the long queue at the check-in counter by Thai International's required time. The queue moved painfully slowly in this laid back and basic airport. Just as we reached the counter, the Thai pilot came out and said, 'No more! Check in time is finished.'

Appalled, we protested that our visas were about to expire and that it was straight to goal for overstaying. To no avail. We were outcast. The kind airport staff tried to help us and eventually found us seats on a flight leaving in a couple of hours with Air Bangladesh. It was the only other flight that day so we took it.

Next time I would choose the Go Straight To Gaol option! It was the worst flight of my life. The plane was old, grubby and much worn. We were the only women aboard not in purdah. The hostesses therefore ignored us as worthless. A male passenger, seeing everyone but us served orange juice, demanded that the hostess give us some. To cap it all off, we almost crashed.

Coming down to land at Bangkok, our plane must have been approaching the wrong landing strip because suddenly the pilot pulled a fast U-turn and took the plane up again. Everything fell about the cabin as it almost turned over. Women screamed and cried. Eventually we made it down to land, but I was much shaken. Never again, that's it for me with Third World airlines, I swore.

In Bangkok we went straight to the agent who had arranged our visas, flights and insurance and got refunds for our unused Thai International tickets, booked more flights and applied for new visas. I think what really happened was that the plane had been overbooked and was full by the time we fronted the counter. I prefer that to the thought that the pilot hadn't liked the look of us.

Three days later we were on our way back to Rangoon. We spent a night at the President Hotel, now the Thamada and also much tarted up. Again we took the Mandalay train north, this time getting off at Thazi – a connecting place for transport en route to Inle Lake. We stayed in Nyaungshwe, the closest village to the lake, and went puttering around this large body of placid water in a motorised canoe. The lake is known for its leg rowers who stand at the back of their canoes and row with one leg wrapped around a single oar.

We saw Pagan's famous temples and took the train back to Rangoon where we stayed at the Kandaggi Hotel – formerly the British Rowing Club, transformed into a guesthouse – on Lake Kandawgyi. Another charmingly ramshackle, rambling old place, delightfully full of character, it looked over the lake to the golden splendour of the Shwedagon Pagoda. It has also gone up in the world and is now the super swish Kandawgyi Palace.

Leaving the country this time, having learned from our previous experience, we arrived at the airport ridiculously early.

The third time I visited Burma, a year later, I was travelling alone. Still allowed only a week's visa, I fitted it in on my way to a month in Nepal. After a night at the Strand I took a ferry across the Yangon River to Syriam, now called Thanlyin. Once a major seaport, it was an interesting place to wander about in.

Then it was a sleeper on the train to Thazi to collect a bus to Kalaw, another former British hill station. Most travellers go to Kalaw because it is a base for treks into the surrounding mountains, but I just investigated the town and its markets where traders come down from hill villages to sell their goods.

One day I went by local transport to a village market some miles away and had to wait a long time at a wayside stop to return, standing under a bamboo shelter with a group of women. A young American man arrived and after a short while began agitating about the delay, and being a bit of a pain. When the bemo arrived, I spoke for the first time and he said in surprise, 'Oh, I thought you were Burmese, you were so quiet.' I was dressed much the same as the local women in a long skirt and over blouse so I suppose this was a reasonable assumption. I climbed into the back of the small covered truck with the women and we sat facing each other in two rows. The boy got up on the roof with a couple of men. Before long we were stopped by soldiers at a road block. I realised then that I should have had a permit to travel into these hills and I began to worry. But when the soldiers looked into the back of the truck, all the women gently swayed forward just a little, like a breeze passing over a wheat field, enough to hide me. Then everyone pointed to the roof. The last I saw of the American boy he was standing in the road yelling at the soldiers.

From Kalaw it wasn't hard to find a couple of travellers to share a taxi back to Rangoon and the Strand for my last night and more drama at the airport. This time it involved an antique tapestry (a *kalaga*) I had bought. Unlike the casual formalities of checking baggage I had seen on my previous visits, this time it looked as though my bag was about to be searched. Suddenly I remembered the *kalaga* – it was forbidden to take antiques out of Burma. Visions of the Go to Gaol clause assailed me and I did some fast thinking. Looking up at the large sign on the wall that stated that no kyat were to be taken out of the country, I feigned surprise and opened my purse to exhibit a wad of it (worth all of five dollars). I said to the customs officer, 'Oh dear. What shall I do with this?' Graciously he said that he would relieve me of it, then he shut my bags and waved me through. I still have that *kalaga* on my wall at home.

For years I was unable to return to Burma. Soon after my last visit in 1988, following non-violent protests in which three thousand people were killed by the military, a coup occurred. The ensuing government established a corrupt and harsh regime that was boycotted by travellers on the advice of Burmese democratic leaders like Aung San Suu Kyi.

Then in 2012 the government began to make concessions towards liberalisation. Elections were held and Aung San Suu Kyi, one of my heroes, changed her mind about the boycott. She said, 'Come, we need your money, but limit the amount that goes to the government by only patronising private hotels and restaurants.' Later, her house arrest was lifted and she was able to leave the country to receive her Nobel Peace Prize.

Time to go back to Burma!

Aung San Suu Kyi and I arrived in Yangon on the same day, only one of us clutching a Nobel Prize unfortunately.

Leaving Adelaide for Burma, I flew first to Darwin to spend three days in my spiritual home, revisiting old friends and haunts. I had dinner at Dinah Beach Cruising Yacht Club where I was delighted to find nothing had changed – the same cook served the same fabulous fish with the same wide smile, breakfast at the Parap market, a Saturday morning tradition, and a barbeque in a balmy, frangipani-scented night. What more could I have asked for?

My soul restored, I left for Singapore in the early evening, switching from Qantas to Jetstar. It took five hours to Singapore. It was a boring, no frills flight but I bought some food and wine to while away the time. The young Irishman sitting next to me had to put his food and beer on my AMEX. Jetstar did not soil their hands with cash.

The onward flight to Rangoon, now known by its pre-colonial name of Yangon, departed in twelve hours so I decided to stay in Changi airport. After being misdirected three times – I don't think even the people who work in this enormous place have any idea what it contains – I found the Transit Hotel. Rooms here are sold in blocks of six hours plus any additional hours required. The accommodation was tiny but well-equipped with TV, phone and air-con, but all the rooms with an ensuite had been taken so I had to wander around the airport corridors to use the bathroom in the fitness centre.

Up early with the wake-up call I had requested, I went in search of my luggage. My bag had not been booked through to Yangon but was being held hostage, awaiting ransom and liberation, in the Lost and Found office.

There was a two hour wait until my flight. I wandered about and ate some awful food – a dish of foul boiled sausages that looked and tasted like entrails. Finally in the departure lounge, I watched two Asian pilots, one a slim young girl, stride past and mount the cockpit of the Jetstar plane waiting outside on the tarmac. On the plane there were four hostesses, two Singaporeans in Jetstar uniforms and two gorgeous Burmese girls in attractive orange *longiis* (a sarong-style long skirt) and blue blouses. My suspicion that this was not a genuine Jetstar flight deepened. The refresher towels handed out as we boarded had first aroused my doubts. Australian airlines gave up such niceties long ago. My misgivings grew when complementary food and drinks were served and I saw the Air Myanmar logos on the food trays. Help! I was flying with a Third World airline again. I had noticed that I was the only Westerner aboard. Was there something I did not know?

On the back of the seat in front of me was a prominently placed brown paper sick bag. It was a long time since I had seen one of those on a plane, and I had never seen one used. Oh well, there's a first time for everything. And Murphy saw to it that the only time I witnessed this event I had a good view of it. I was seated beside the thrower-upperer. The poor woman used that bag with a will, including while my food tray was in front of me. Not that it deterred me.

The flight from Singapore to Yangon took two and a half hours. When the Burmese woman next to me managed to get her head out of the sick bag for long enough to fill out her immigration form she asked me for help. I tried. But she could possibly be in prison by now! I have no Burmese and she had no English.

At Yangon airport, despite the new terminal, it was the remembered humid, sticky, noisy, crowded chaos. A plane from Bangkok had arrived at the same time, bringing a few back-packers. We all gravitated to a pair of young men who were enticingly waving a placard labelled 'Motherland Guesthouse'. I had made a booking there, I hoped. It had been difficult to find places that could take an internet booking or even that had internet access.

The Motherland welcome committee said they did not have a booking registered for me but they took me with them anyway. We stood outside the building waiting for their van for what seemed an age, sweating amid the surrounding bedlam. Finally the van came but there was not enough room for all of us so an English lad and I were shunted off in a rattly old taxi. It took an hour to reach the guesthouse and I arrived steaming and panting for the cold drink that was offered. An air-conned taxi was a rarity in Yangon.

I had recognised nothing on the drive. There seemed to be a lot more cars and the traffic was mad, but at least there were not the blaring horns of Bangkok.

chapter 2

At Motherland chaos reigned supreme. The tiny foyer was packed with new arrivals, most of whose bookings appeared to have been lost like mine. I was finally found a room. This guesthouse is extremely popular thanks to Lonely Planet's endorsement. (Which, incidentally, turned out to be well deserved.) The staff was unbelievably kind and patient. Nothing was too much trouble.

My room was a pleasant surprise. Big, with lots of light via almost two walls of windows, it had an attached, perfectly adequate bathroom with touchingly innocent faults like a towel rail you'd have to have been ten feet tall to reach. And if that didn't deter you, it was placed directly under the aim of the shower water. The toilet system was unable to cope with toilet paper so the roll of paper was lovingly enshrined in a plastic case and displayed like the treasure it is on the table beside the bed, nowhere near the loo. The paper was wound into its case so that it came out furled like a flag and needed to be unravelled to make it usable. Was this just to make life interesting? The way the zoo keeps orangutans mentally active by hiding their food. There were two three-quarter sized beds, comfortable if hard, an air-con that worked well – when the power was on (it failed regularly). A TV hung from the ceiling of the alcove between the entrance and bathroom doors, so high and in such an awkward position that it was almost impossible to see, so it was a good thing it didn't work.

I was very happy with my room's outlook. One window

provided a panoramic view of a stone wall, but the other looked out over the narrow alley behind the guesthouse where the cook house lived partly covered by a slanting corrugated-iron roof. Here, against either wall of the alley, big aluminium cauldrons perched on braziers and steam rose from pots cooking on hot plates on low tables. The kitchen may not have been five star but the food it produced was delicious and freshly cooked.

Work began early down there in the cook house, and, after a great sleep, I lay in the pre-dawn light listening to the sounds that rose up to me – voices chatting quietly, roosters crowing, cheeping chickens, a cat calling to her mewing kittens, and someone playing softly on a flute.

Presenting myself for breakfast downstairs in the guesthouse restaurant, an attendant sang softly to himself as he brought me a tray of white bread and jam. This may be considered a delicacy here, but not by me. I rejected it politely and asked for eggs. An omelette filled with vegetables, two sweet, tree-ripened bananas and a mug of wonderful local coffee replaced the first offering.

The Motherland staff took their obligation to feed you breakfast very seriously. You were almost force fed it. No matter what time you left in the morning it was compulsory first to have breakfast. I even saw it offered to folk who had just arrived as they waited for their rooms. As a lifelong devotee of a good breakfast, how could I not have fallen in love with people so dedicated to it?

I spent the morning in a fruitless search for onward travel by river. Burma is well supplied with rivers, and boats have always been used as a means of transport around the country. Since roads have been built the opportunity for passenger travel on boats has decreased. I had seen a boat trip up the famous Irrawaddy River advertised in an Adelaide newspaper and asked about this. Strangely, no one had heard of it in Burma. But the patience of the girls at Motherland who helped me look for it was limitless. They phoned and used the internet but all the phone numbers recorded for this establishment had been changed, were wrong or did not answer. This was not uncommon. The phone service here was notoriously deficient.

After a terrific lunch of fish, ginger and onions, I walked around the corner to a shop I had been told sold mobile phones. On the way I walked over a railway line that passed between tumbledown shops and buildings and crossed the road without signs or barriers. In my room I had heard trains hooting as they went very slowly past. It was absolutely essential to go slowly, I thought, after seeing the way people walked all over the line. I wondered how many people the train caught unawares.

In the phone shop an obliging young woman inserted a SIM card into my phone for me. It cost a mere twenty three dollars and came with ten dollars worth of credit. Later I found my phone was blocked and did not work. I returned and discovering that I could not get a refund so I bought another phone! Me! Luddite of the Year with two phones. But it was a bright classy red and only cost another twenty dollars, considerably cheaper than a short while ago when severe restrictions on mobile phones existed and just a SIM card cost around a thousand dollars!

Then I took a taxi to the town centre. It wasn't far and taxis were fairly cheap; it cost about three dollars. Yangon, bordered on the south and west by the Yangon River, is Burma's largest city and was its capital from British rule in 1885 through to independence in 1948 until 2005 when the government built a new city at Nay Pi Taw in central Burma and suddenly announced that poor old Yangon had been demoted. There seems to have been no logical explanation for this move, although it is said to have been advised by government sanctioned fortune tellers.

Yangon's downtown streets were as appalling as the area around Motherland – broken and dirty. When I stopped to give an old beggar woman a donation – the only beggar I saw incidentally – a large and muscular rat, the Mike Tyson of rats, ran over my feet and shot off down the gutter.

I came upon a small supermarket on my travels and ambled around it casually, much to the suspicion of the many security guards who followed behind keeping me under surveillance. The owners of this establishment had missed the point of supermarkets being self-service. Along one wall stocked with cosmetics, maybe fifteen feet in length, six female assistants stood ready to help you. Unfortunately, it was impossible to see the goods past the barrier they presented. However, I did find a thirty cent electricity adapter plug.

Not surprisingly, in the confusing central area of Yangon I didn't locate the place I had been given directions to, but I did manage to find my way back to Motherland on foot.

A handy landmark of inner Yangon is the Sule Pagoda, whose great golden stupa rises incongruously from among government buildings and shops at the centre of the town's primary traffic intersection. It is thought to be two thousand years old and to enshrine a sacred hair relic of the Buddha.

A total of three hours hiking about in the heat had almost finished me. Thank heaven for my brollie. It was now July and the rainy season, and although not the hottest time of the year, it wasn't the coolest either. I fell into my room pooped and soaked, wringing wet with sweat. I had a cold shower and gave up on this day after phoning all over town seeking a room for tomorrow. I had to leave Motherland then as they were fully booked. The reception staff helped me and eventually I found a vacancy in a hotel closer to the centre called the Queen's Park.

Checkout time in Burma is a civilised twelve midday, so that's when I moved on. My new hotel had a grand-looking exterior, albeit no sign of a park, nor the queen for that matter. At the front desk two charming receptionists gradually overcame their surprise at seeing that I was Western, female and alone, and decided which room would suit me. I paid a little more for a superior room, at the front with lots of light.

The hotel had a cavernous empty dining room where I had lunch after making a spectacular entrance. I missed the bottom step and performed a four-point landing splat onto the hard concrete floor. Two waiters rushed to scrape me up and restore me to a more dignified position. The food cost much the same as at the Motherland. I was to find prices the same all over the country no matter where I ate, in seedy work men's cafes or hotels.

One of the front desk receptionists spoke some English and she helped me find an address for the agent of the *Pandaw*, the elusive boat that allegedly sailed the Irrawaddy. After several unsuccessful phone attempts I set off in a taxi to find it. It was situated a couple of miles north of the city centre at the Inya Lake Hotel.

What a ride! In a death-defying taxi with no windows, I was flown along the roads in a howling gale. Horrible. I sat directly behind the driver hoping he would act as an air bag when the inevitable collision came. In that position I couldn't see the worst that was happening around us, like pedestrians peeling off our fenders. Managing speeds of one hundred plus whenever possible, the driver weaved madly all over the road, in and out of phalanxes of buses and cars.

We reached Inya Lake much to my relief. This extensive lake is off limits at places where there are state guesthouses or ministerial housing. At one end is the home of Aung San Suu Kyi where she had spent much of the past twenty years under house arrest.

At the Inya Lake Hotel, a very posh hotel with a grand foyer, the receptionist imparted the unwelcome news that the *Pandaw* office was no longer there. They had moved last week, pushed by Murphy no doubt. The lengths some people will go to avoid me. The receptionist obligingly phoned around searching for the firm – they had left no forwarding address – and eventually sent me off in another taxi. This one dumped me at a big building where I wandered from dreary semi-lit floor to floor until another kind woman took me in tow and delivered me to an office. I was shown into a waiting room obviously meant for VIPs. It was packed with heavily carved wooden furniture, including seven enormous blue velvet upholstered thrones arranged along one wall. Another lovely young woman explained that I was still not in the right place for this by now apparently mythical boat.

She wrote down the address I needed and outside the building I found a taxi driver who, with the help of several passersby acting as interpreters, said he knew the way. He didn't. He took me up and down unlikely looking lanes and tried to deposit me several times at various doorways. We finally arrived at a place with a guard who said, yes, this was the place, and I got out.

Now a second security guard appeared. He said, no, this was not the number that was written on my piece of paper. He pointed down the road and I set off on foot. After walking for some distance and finding nothing likely, I returned to the gate where I accosted a passing schoolboy who led me to the building I wanted. I wondered how you could stand all day at a gate and not know which numbers were along your street.

Finally I climbed a steep narrow flight of the grittiest broken stairs imaginable to the office of the agent. But it was all to no avail. The boat had no booking or shipping facilities in Burma – it was all done from Australia by email. But yet another sympathetic woman took my phone number for future contact. I returned, exhausted, for dinner at the QPH and a rest. The TV in my room had CNN so I put my feet up and watched the news.

All accommodation in Burma seemed to provide breakfast in the room rate, probably a legacy of the British B & B tradition. The QPH's was buffet style in the dining room, with a good selection of fruit, juice, great coffee and Asian dishes, even eggs if ordered. Most other patrons of the hotel seemed to be Asian businessmen and I was the only Westerner.

The phone in my room was easy to use, even if the numbers were hit and miss, either disconnected or changed. I got travel agents from the phone book and called several until I found one who spoke enough English to understand what I wanted – to travel by boat. He was very helpful and told me about the local boat that went around the delta to Pathein. It seemed to be the only possibility at that time. I had given up on the *Pandaw*.

Once more the receptionists at the front desk phoned for directions, put me in a taxi, and waved me off to the ticket office for the local delta boat. They told me I looked Burmese, which I took as a compliment.

chapter 3

At the shipping office on a riverside wharf I was ushered into a tin shed that was the waiting room for boat travellers. It was filled to the brim with people sitting on benches or their luggage, but I was shooed through this place and installed in the manager's small office. It was very hot in there but at least I had a proper chair. I was told to wait thirty minutes. At ten the manager arrived. So much for early Asian starts to the day.

This nice man showed me a photo of the boat and promised me a cabin. As a foreigner I had to pay a much inflated price in dollars but he could not change my hundred dollar note. I signed an agreement to accept the cabin and to pay for both berths when I came to board the ship at three the next day for a five o'clock sailing. My passport was inspected, all my details were recorded in a book, and I was free to go.

The day before when I had been speaking to the woman who told me about the *Pandaw*, she had mentioned this local boat trip to Pathein. She said that the *Pandaw* had not been able to obtain a license to travel this route because of the danger of going out to sea in a large bay that can be wild at times. Now it occurred to me that the *Pandaw* looked much bigger and better than the riverboat on which I was about to venture out there.

The taxi driver who had been waiting for me took me to the street of opticians where I ordered a pair of specs to be made to the prescription I had brought with me. The frame I chose was branded Chanel but I very much doubt it, and the whole arrangement cost twenty-eight dollars. I also ordered some new prescription lens for my sunglasses. They cost an unbelievable nine dollars. The three staff spoke little English and it was not easy, but very pleasant, doing business with them. Many times they tried to force cold drinks and coffee on me. The specs turned out to be good. They told me I was very pretty. Was I back in You Are Very Beautiful Country or were they in need of some of their products? Maybe it was just my lipstick.

From this street it was a short walk to the huge Bogeye Market, known formerly as Scott's Market. Both sides of the road it faces are solidly fenced and the only access to it is via a high overpass approached by a wide set of steps. On the overpass three old beggars sat at intervals – one man and two women. I gave them all a contribution. On my way back I was appalled to see a foreign man photographing one of the old women, shoving a huge telephoto lens into her face. Outraged, I berated him for his insensitivity. He looked embarrassed. I am not sure he understood what I said, but there was no mistaking the content. Walking on, I passed the other old woman and she gave me a conspiratorial smile and wave.

On the ground floor, inside the main entrance of the extensive market, were many jewellery stalls. Most of them stocked over-the-top pieces decorated with rubies, sapphires and other precious stones. Burmese rubies have always been considered the world's best and I wouldn't say no to a bucketful of any of the other gems either. There were also stalls belonging to goldsmiths, devoted only to gold jewellery.

I bought a sandalwood fan from a young girl who was walking about offering them and a *longii*, the ankle-length skirt worn by all local women. The traditional ones are woven and the material is fairly heavy and stiff, too hot for me in this climate. I bought a lighter polyester sort, and a pair of scuffs. The shoes I was wearing were about to die. They would not be going home with me.

I saw two tourists in the market. There were not many around the town. Last evening I had passed another two on the street, but, apart from those at Motherland, these were the only Western foreigners I saw the entire time I was in Yangon.

Then I went looking for lunch. I had not lost my usual enthusiastic appetite, but, fortunately in view of the lack of public conveniences, I had lost the need for loos. You sweat excess fluid out instead.

In a nearby street I found an Indian working man's cafe and sat down at a communal metal table. This place was alive with activity. All the cooking was done at the entrance in huge pots or on grills. It looked very down market and I was an oddity, foreign as well as a woman.

I ate a bowl of sweet and sour chicken and it was great – the same as in the QPH only with more frills. I got several side dishes of carrots, cucumbers and onions.

I gave to two more beggars. A young man without legs and a young woman sitting with two small children on the steps of an overpass. Her naked children looked sick and she did not ask, just looked in my eyes.

Taxiing the short distance back to the hotel cost a couple of dollars. It beat walking in the heat. After a rest, I went off to collect my new glasses that had only taken a few hours to produce. Then I walked down to the market along a street, the pavements of which were now lined with evening street sellers, spilling out onto the road almost into the traffic. There was a lively mob looking at mobile phones. Then came a stretch where sellers of used books had set their wares out on blankets on the footpath. I spied George Orwell's *Burmese Days* and snapped it up for a couple of dollars. William Arthur Blair, as he really was, lived for many years in Burma (his family were here for generations) and wrote *Burmese Days*, his first novel, while living in Kachan.

Further on were sellers of all manner of mechanical bits and pieces. I bought a small pair of long-nosed pliers for a few cents. I had forgotten to bring mine. Those and a tiny screwdriver are essential equipment for a Travelling Plumber as well as for fixing all manner of problems like broken suitcase handles.

By now I was beginning to get my bearings and I knew that if I walked back along this road I would hopefully come to my hotel. It was a long way among the evening crowds, but I had all the stalls to divert me. Dark clouds were gathering and a cool wind, a harbinger of coming rain, brought relief. I bought bananas, yoghurt and cheese from sellers along the way, and that was dinner.

Later that evening I watched from the wide window of my fourth floor room as a terrific storm blew in, bringing heavy rain that pelted down for hours.

After another fine breakfast I tried the hotel's internet room, but the internet was missing in action. Murphy got there first. So I read the paper in the foyer and had lunch in the dining room to fill in time until I could take a taxi to the shipping office. There, the manager produced the two tickets for my cabin, shook my hand and sent me off with two bearers of my luggage. I followed these jaunty boys out along the wharf and onto the boat where they dumped my stuff in my cabin. A big wooden barrier stood across the steps that led up from the lower deck to the cabin deck. A gent who looked like the purser examined my ticket and let me pass. I gave the porters their agreed fee. At least there were no arguments here when a price has been settled. It was the same with taxis, none of whom had meters, but it would be a trap for the unwary to ride in one without first setting a price.

The cabin was superficially clean but oh so care-worn and

shabby! There were stains galore from the mould and heat of the tropics. There were two beds, each with a pillow and a blanket, a table between them, a fan, and a window each side of the door that opened onto the deck outside. The windows had insect screens, adequately supplied with holes big enough to allow the mosquitoes in, while the holes in the screen covering the door were big enough to let in a horse. I had to sleep with everything shut to avoid malaria. The purser/attendant came along and sprayed my cabin heavily with insect spray, which almost did for me never mind the mosquitoes. I escaped out onto the deck to let it settle. He then produced a sturdy bright green plastic stool for me to sit on. The breeze on deck was a relief.

The port was excitingly busy. Another ferry was double parked alongside us and I watched people coming and going from it, unloading their cargo of sacs of rice. The cargo for our boat was being carried on men's shoulders from the waterside, through open wooden hatchways in the deck, down into the hold below.

The boat had three decks including the one I was on. The cabins occupied one end and the other consisted of open space containing rows of wooden chairs for deck passengers. Between where the stairs came up were two small rooms – a toilet and a shower. They were both secured with padlocks to which I was given a key. The third deck above me was the top deck, with the captain's quarters, the bridge and more deck passenger space.

Shortly the attendant produced a large bottle of water for me and said I could order a meal from him too if I got hungry. A young man who spoke some English came to chat to me. He was seeing his girlfriend off and said she would look after me if I needed any help. I was the only foreigner aboard and I didn't find anyone else who spoke English.

I was sitting on the deck reading a book and waiting for the boat to leave when I heard myself addressed. Looking up I felt a jolt of fear as I saw a stern face and a police uniform. I was about to be interrogated! I had to state my name, nationality and destination. I smiled a lot and tried to look harmless. I seemed to pass inspection and the police moved on searching for more suspicious characters trying to flee to the countryside.

chapter 4

Around five o'clock, pretty much on the scheduled time, two loud blasts of the horn announced our departure. We edged away from the wharf and inched our way out into the stream of the Yangon River. Loaded to the gunwales with cargo and deck and cabin passengers, we set off towards the setting sun, now partly obscured by dark clouds.

The trip down the Yangon River to the Bay of Martaban took several hours. Soon it was dark and there was nothing else to see so I went to bed. I made a toilet call beforehand and entered the door on which was, I thought, a sign that read toilet. Inside there was only a big metal tub of very brown river water, a plastic dipper, a lot of rusting pipes, and a hole in the floor. Confused, I used the floor and did a lot of sluicing. Coming out I met the purser who pointed out to me that the loo was next door. I think the sign on the door must have said bathroom. How embarrassment!

I was asleep when, around eleven, we stopped at a town and much noise and activity followed. Cargo and passengers came and went. I slept again. There was no swell and the boat made little movement. I had expected more especially after we reached the bay.

Around dawn we stopped at another town. The delta region now was on both sides of us. Largely uninhabited, everything was very green, mostly low trees and palms, although now and then I saw rice paddies. When there was a house, it was rustic – built of wood and bamboo – sometimes with a boat tied to a pole beside it. The river craft we passed were many and varied – small wooden skiffs rowed by a man standing on a raised rear platform using a pair of oars crossed over in front of him, long barges low in the water with freight, big motorised canoes with lines of passengers sitting in them, and large riverboats similar to ours.

An hour later we stopped in another town and there was the usual bustle of freight and passengers coming on and getting off the ship. In mid morning we stopped at another town where small boys swam around us. I thought we had arrived. The young girl who had been appointed my guardian came to say goodbye and wish me happy travels as this was her home town. She told me that Pathein was another two or three hours away yet.

It was a long but pleasant trip with a lot to see. I could lie on my bed and watch the passing scene through the open door, or sit on the deck on my plastic stool. Then the boat entered the Pathein River, one of the many mouths of the Irrawaddy that make up the delta and slowly navigated up it to Pathein town. It became hotter as we chugged along at low speed, and heavy clouds moved in threatingly. The Irrawaddy is one of three big rivers that run through Burma. One of the most navigable rivers in Asia, it enters the sea here at the Bay of Bengal.

At three in the afternoon we arrived at Pathein, known as Bassein in the time of the British. The centre of a major rice growing area, it is Myanmar's fourth biggest city and the most important river port outside Yangon.

I hired two of the porters who had surged aboard looking for custom. They took charge of me and my bag and bundled us into two trishaws, after first herding me into the immigration office on the wharf to have my details recorded.

It was either motorbike or pedal power here. There were no taxis. My entourage pedalled off. It wasn't far to the La Pyat

Wun, the hotel I had booked with my new mobile. It was okay, but considering it was supposedly the best accommodation in town, it was nowhere near flash. The staff was nice though.

I was shown one room with a window that looked onto a wall and asked for another. The second was better and had much more light. I had to forgo hot water for the light though. This floor was too high for the hot water to reach. Whatever. Who needs hot water when the weather is so hot? The first thing I did was take a shower, cold or not. Walking up the street afterwards I passed many shopfronts hung with the umbrellas and beautiful hand-painted parasols of all colours and sizes that Pathein is famous for. An umbrella aficionado, I was in heaven. There were even shops where umbrella menders sat repairing them.

Then I went looking for food, which developed into a quest that wasn't all that easy. The hotel had no restaurant and finding a place to eat was a problem. But finally I came across a sort of cafe where I persuaded the cook/proprietor to feed me. It took some convincing that what I wanted was food. I wonder what he thought I was there for – sitting at a table, napkin at the ready, bib tied on, knife and fork clutched in hand, and salivating! There was no menu. With a lot of pantomime I managed to get through that I would eat chicken. Big mistake. I had not noticed as I came in from the street that in the open shopfront there was a glass case containing lumps of unidentifiable meat that had obviously sat there all day in the heat. It turned out to be the aforementioned chicken and this was to what the cook now applied his attentions. Extracting an unsavoury looking chunk of this roadkill, he moved to a nearby piece of sawn-off tree stump that served as a chopping block and gave it a good seeing to with a cleaver.

The resulting unappealing mess was taken away out the back somewhere. After a long time, a huge pile of greyish noodles topped with a couple of quail eggs for good measure was plonked in front of me. It didn't taste too bad but it wasn't too good either. Worried about the gastro I was risking, I asked for a beer hoping to maybe disinfect my stomach with alcohol. They had no beer but I had noticed in Burma that no one will say they don't have an item – they just send a boy off to get it. So in time a can of Myanmar beer was produced. As beer goes it was perfectly acceptable.

While I sat there eating in the open front of the café it began to rain heavily and I watched sheets of water deluging down, cascading off the roof of a shop across the way, hitting its plastic awning, pouring into a bucket inadequately trying to collect the runoff. This ended the day for me. I slept as soon as I went to bed until a pack of dogs woke me howling and fighting in the street under my window. There were lots of dogs everywhere I went in Burma and most seemed not to belong to anyone.

After slowly getting up the next morning I set off in search of breakfast. Black coffee turned out to be a rarity. Three places I tried attempted to give me packets of the abominable three in one – coffee, milk and sugar. I'd sooner take poison. The owner of the place where I had eaten last night gave me a smile and a wave as I went past. How could he forget me? Wherever I went I was regarded as an oddity.

After a long walk and lots of attempts, I found a restaurant, or so it was labelled. Here I was fed a huge plate of noodles mixed with various bits and pieces, and, after three attempts, I did get some proper local black coffee.

From Pathein I decided to travel west by bus to a beach on the Bay of Bengal. With the aid of my hotel's lovely receptionist, I went in a trishaw to the bus station. Everyone denied that the bus station was where the guide book vowed it was – instead I was taken in quite another direction. Located in a muddy swamp, the ticket office (a rough wooden box) lurked amid dilapidated old buses. Here I was given the unpleasant information that there was no air-con bus. The signs I had seen advertising these buses in the main street were only for the Yangon bus. I asked for the other bus station but was told that this was it. There was no other. I didn't believe them. I set off again on foot following the directions I had been given to a place that served lunch. It was a long way and all my wanderings thus far had been performed in spitting rain.

When I found the lunch place, I was happy to find it had good food. There was even a menu. I ordered hot and sour chicken. Reading the list of chicken dishes, one item stopped me in my tracks – 'Fried Person's Nose'. The 'Next Pig's Ear' was also a bit curious.

My guide book map showed their alleged bus station close to where I was then, so I decided to walk there. Coming across the local police station, I stopped and asked a group of young men outside it – isn't anyone old in this country? – the way. They conferred and sent me off again. Following their directions I ended up back at the first bus station where I had to shamefacedly admit that they had been right. There was no other bus station.

Sloshing and squelching – do not bring your best shoes to Burma – through black horrible mud to the wooden hutch of an office, I negotiated for a seat on a bus to the beach at Ngwe Saung. They showed me the bus in question as it stood in the yard. It was no Greyhound but it looked reasonable. Though I guessed it would not be so good looking by the time it had been loaded with cargo and people. I was also shown a seating plan, and, hopefully, was reserved two seats – one for me and one for my bag.

I trishawed back to the hotel. The rider and I agreed on his asking price of five hundred but it was so much work for him in the muddy broken streets that when I got there I gave him the five, then took it back and gave him a thousand. The smile split his face. Now he is sure all foreigners are quite mad. A whole thousand! Diamond Jim I am not. This was the equivalent of ninety cents.

Then it was R & R after a cold shower – this was the time to have it, hot and sticky after several hours outside. Later, with more directions to another restaurant, which I found after only one false start, I ordered a dish of chicken with bamboo shoots that managed to transform themselves into carrots between the menu and the plate.

The next morning it was not so hard to find breakfast, but I had to give up and drink poisonously sweet milk coffee as I ate two plates of unidentifiable stuff rolled in batter. After a leisurely pack, I discovered to my amazement that this out-of-the-way place had free wifi. I used it down in the lobby (it, like the hot water, didn't climb stairs) until it was time to leave for the bus. At this exact moment a storm blew up and it started to rain, but with the aid of two trishaws my bag and I made it to the bus station relatively dry.

To my surprise my seat had been reserved and I had no hassles fighting people off it. The bus left only half an hour late and only two passengers had to sit in the aisle. My seat was in the front close behind the driver. It was a bench seat and really only big enough for one person by Western standards. The driver and I were separated by a bit of waist-high battered tin. My bag was put half out of the open window next to me on the seat. It was good that the rain had stopped now. Everyone on the bus gaped at me when I got on, but I faced them and said '*Minggala ba*' (hello, blessings), and received smiles and replies in response. A latecomer indicated that my seat needed another occupant but was told by the other passengers, I think, that I had paid for it. (Or perhaps that I had a communicable disease.) Whatever, I was left alone.

On the front seat opposite me sat a Burmese man who seemed to be trading and delivering stuff along the way. I saw him handing parcels over and collecting money. When he got on the bus he had shooed off a woman already sitting on the seat and the poor woman then had to travel squatting on the tiniest wooden stool I have ever seen, just five centimetres off the ground. Later a sack of rice was loaded on and she sat on that.

The driver was an exact copy of one of those bald laughing Buddha statues. He even had the same curious curled-up earlobes. Taking off, we squelched out of the mud pack that was the station yard and very, very slowly crawled along the ruts of the so-called road beside the river. The road continued like this for kilometres with the town spread out along it, consisting mostly low one-storey buildings interspersed with the odd pagoda. When I had been told that this trip of forty eight kilometres took two and a half hours I had wondered why. Now I knew. Take a terrible road one car wide, a decrepit bus full to the brim with sacks of rice, baskets of produce and as many Burmese as could be squeezed on (plus one foreigner), then add a whole pile of steep mountains, winding tracks and goods and people to pick up and drop off along the way, and two and a half hours seemed about right.

The country we travelled through was beautiful and so green, with rice paddies and a lot of water. We went up and down mountains with little sign of habitation except the occasional incredibly ramshackle wooden dwelling that was more a hut than a house. I took only one photo, of a WWII army truck that was a glorious, unbelievable wreck but still in use. An Australian RTA inspection unit could have spent a week defaulting it.

Now and then I saw the bus driver take a wad of betel nut and pop it in his mouth – hopefully not to put him into too tranquil a state on these precipitous hillsides. Sitting as I was directly behind him, after a while I had the feeling that something did not quite feel right. I could not work out what was wrong until I realised that he should have been on the other side of the bus. They drive on the left of the road in Burma but the bus was a right-hand drive vehicle.

My arrival in Ngwe Saung was painless. Fighting off the proffered motorbike, I showed the address of the guesthouse

I had chosen to a boy who summoned two trishaws and for the agreed price of one thousand each we set off on what must surely have been the most picturesque ride of my life. I was pedalled along the edge of a marvellous beach fringed and shaded by coconut palms, while on the other side of the narrow road the jungle crowded down thickly. Every now and then we passed a few bungalows of a guest house or resort. It was cool and the road was a narrow, paved strip – fortunately almost all flat for the poor boys pedalling. But it was a long way, at least a couple of kilometres.

The guesthouse Shwe Hin Tha sat smack on the sand, the reception desk in an open-sided thatched-roof pavilion. The nearby accommodation was a row of bamboo bungalows. I chose one only ten paces from where the waves broke on the shore.

I was immensely comfortable there. The breeze off the sea kept the heat down, the room was big and the bathroom Spartan, but I had everything I could want except full-time electricity, which came on from six in the evening until ten. And when it came on, it did so with a bang. The room was suddenly brilliantly flood-lit by a big globe that seemed to attempt to make up for its former absence with its brightness.

My room had a covered porch fringed by palm trees that faced the waves curling on the sand. It was outfitted with heavy wooden chairs and a big low table. As I sat there, a girl came by to ask if I needed anything. I enquired about food and a much-needed meal of hot and sour fish was brought to me promptly. Unfortunately I had forgotten to ask if the fish came complete. It did. I got the whole shooting match – bones, head, tail, eyes and all – tasty but hard work. I thought it strange that there were no seagulls here but lots of dark, chirping hopping birds like minors came begging when they saw that I had food.

Then I had a great siesta. Towards dark, another girl wielding fly spray called in and also lit some mosquito coils. Shortly after the water was hot enough for a much-needed shower and hair wash. I need not have worried about the state of my hairdo as it was blown all over the place immediately by the constant breeze.

I went to bed, all night in my sleep blissfully aware of the rolling surf and the voice of the sea.

chapter 5

It was pouring rain when I woke in the morning which made it pleasantly cool. Breakfast was served in the restaurant, another thatched, open-sided shelter a short step way on the sand.

A group of young Burmese came to use the bungalow next to mine. One girl appeared at my open door, then came inside. Although she could not communicate with me in any way, she stood close to me, staring. I went out onto the porch and she followed and sat next to me. Eventually I had to go for a walk to lose her. It was as though she saw me as a sideshow entertainment. Or maybe she thought I needed company after discovering that I was alone.

I sat on my porch reading George Orwell's *Burmese Days*. What a great writer. And how good to find his book on Burma to read while in the country. I spent several restful days in this delightful spot. Walking to meals was the only effort I made.

On the third day the sky became overcast right down to the sea with the darkest, blackest clouds. Then the rain came in with a roar across the Bay of Bengal and the waves of the pale-green sea rose up into rows of white-capped rollers. All day a terrific wind blew and heavy rain fell on and off. The little island that sat topped by trees close offshore was obliterated by rain and dense, black cloud. Nothing could be heard above the boom of the wild, grey-green white-foamed breakers as they crashed onto the sand.

At dinner I asked for a banana but was told they didn't have any. I ordered chicken. The waiter returned and told me that the chicken was 'No good'. I presumed from the way he said this that it had gone bad – past its use by date. At least I wasn't given it. At breakfast I tried again for a banana and was told again, 'No got'. Then I was offered banana pancake. This, he said, was okay. The pancake came, sans banana, but was still called banana pancake.

Returning from breakfast, outside my bungalow I found the cleaner trying unsuccessfully to fit into my shoes – footwear lives outside everywhere in Burma. She laughed and came to measure her feet against mine, amused that my feet were so small. At lunch I met a nice lad from New Zealand who had walked down the beach from another guesthouse and had my first English conversation since arriving in Burma while we waited for the current deluge to pass.

I was pleasantly surprised to find that here the guesthouse management did not frown upon clothes washing. They positively encouraged it. For the first time the freebies in the bathroom included a small packet of washing detergent. I appreciated the thought, but the goo was pretty useless – it was the consistency of toothpaste and about as much use on your clothes. However, I used it and departed a Good, Clean Little Tourist.

Another great storm rose up that day and by dark the wind was howling as if a cyclone was coming. The manager reassured me that it was not now cyclone time, merely the rainy season. Still, by the middle of the night I was actually fearful that the roof might blow off. I had never heard rain like that before and I have lived through several near cyclones in the north-west of Australia. From the news reports I had heard I assumed that this band of weather was the edge of a cyclone that had recently devastated Japan and southern China.

By the morning I was sick of the wind, but it was no longer raining, just grey and wild. Breakfast was toast and eggs. I was asked how I wanted my eggs – scrambled, fried or omelette. I said omelette. I got scrambled. I had come to realise that I got what they wanted to give me. However, a banana now came unrequested, two days late.

I found the manager, a personable young man, in the reception area. He told me that my guide book was wrong about the return buses to Yangon. The writer had failed to notice that the bus times quoted were only for the dry season. Now, in the rainy season, there was only one bus a week except for a local one to Pathein that left at 6.30 am. This would mean getting up in the dark (no lights). Anyway, it was out of the question for someone who considers nine am to be the crack of dawn. He tried to find a share taxi for me but there were few travellers around at present, only some Burmese and a pair of Germans at another guesthouse. The manager's tiny cat came to inspect me. She was not at all like the cats we call Burmese in Australia. She was fawn coloured with darker face markings. Satisfied that I was not a threat, mother cat then brought her four microscopic kittens to meet me too. I gave up on the sharing idea and asked the manager to organise a taxi to Pathein for the following day. From there, I would get a bus back to Yangon.

The taxi came at eleven next morning, a modern 4WD that could have taken five people. Blow those tight backpackers who wouldn't pay a third of the fare. So in solitary state I set off for Pathein. Shortly we passed the turn off to the elephant camp I had read about. Although Burma has the world's largest population of working elephants, this was only a tourist place so I let it pass.

It was a pleasant ride back to Pathein and the driver looked after me well. Arriving in the town he took me to a shop to have my passport photocopied three times – the front page and the visas and especially the page with my next of kin. Were they expecting to lose me? I was leaving a paper trail across this land and being monitored all the way, that's for sure. The bus driver took these photocopies and gave one set to the checkpoint officer each time we left or entered the three districts we passed through on the way to Yangon.

The bus was a big surprise and so was the bus company office. This was a new company operating at reduced prices in order to get custom. My ticket cost three thousand kyats, about three dollars. For this I was given a bottle of water, a banana and an air-con waiting room with a proper toilet. We were ferried from the office to the bus station and bundled into the posh Yangon bus – the luggage even went underneath it and not in the aisles for everyone to clamber over.

I was the only foreigner. I sat next to a middle-aged Burmese gentleman who greeted me politely. Halfway to Yangon the bus stopped for food and comforts. I followed a line of women heading, I hoped, for the toilet. It was an oriental squat affair and now I saw the value of wearing a *longii*. Hitch it up and it keeps out of the grot, unlike trousers that have to go down and are in danger of mixing with it.

We had left on time and so arrived at the prescribed hour in Yangon, but then I found that the bus station is way out of town, strangely and inconveniently positioned an hour's ride from the city. By the time I made it into the welcoming arms of Motherland, where I had a booking, it was dark.

The room I was given this time was similar to the one I'd had before, but it had better views from the windows. Now I had trees (almost my favourite things) to look at, as well as a large rubbish heap (not high on the list) that people came to fossick in. I washed and had a much-needed meal of chicken and vegetables. Apart from the banana the bus had provided I had not eaten since eight that morning.

It rained heavily during the night but was steaming hot again the next morning. I taxied to the railway station. I know that buying a train ticket gives money to the crap government but it was only fourteen dollars. I wanted now to travel around the Gulf of Martaban in the opposite direction from where I had just been on the delta. My aim was the town of Moulmein, capital of the Mon State in south-west Burma where 75 per cent of people are Mon. I would like to have gone by boat but foreigners were not allowed to travel this way.

What a great echoing cavern the covered shed that was the Yangon railway station turned out to be. It had absolutely acres of free space and lots of counters manned by platoons of staff, but there were no customers except me rattling around in there – possibly because buses are not government owned and are much cheaper. Not to mention that trains are said to be dangerous, derailments occur in wet weather, and the occasional one is still blown up by people who are peeved with the government.

In the middle of all this empty space a man sat at a small rickety wooden table decorated with a tin teapot, a china cup and an exercise book. Above him a big sign said, 'Complaints'. Oh yair! Who would be game to complain here? And an exercise book! Any complaints could be erased easily.

I asked directions of one man behind a ticket counter and was sent to another way down the line. I eventually garnered the unwelcome information that there were no sleeper trains and that the latest daytime train departed at 7.15 am. After much deliberation I opted for that. I would have to break my rule of dawn being at nine just this once. I had to give the teller fifteen instead of fourteen dollars as he did not have a dollar change. I guessed that they did not do much trade with foreigners, the only passengers who had to pay in dollars.

From the station it was only a short walk to Bogeye Market. I needed to change some money and the money changers there are reliable, quick and give the best rates. In the street of opticians, an Indian man accosted me and tried to lure me into his shop. When I said that what I needed was a battery for my watch, he took me to a shop that did this. My watch had died the minute it hit the tropics.

After walking in the wrong direction for a while I gave up on the attempt to find my own way back to Motherland and hailed a taxi.

I watched the rain pouring down all through lunch, but then it slackened to a light sprinkling, so I set off again. As soon as I was well away from cover the rain immediately increased to a torrential downpour. Despite my umbrella I was soon drenched, wet through to my skin, even my underwear was soaked. I took refuge under a tree, then a bridge, but the rain still kept up. Finally, I made it to the shopping centre I had been heading for that I had been told was just around the corner. It was, but I went around the wrong corner, did my usual thing and got hopelessly lost. At the heavily security guarded door, I squelched inside, dripping onto their nice clean floor. With the soaked *longii* stuck to my legs binding my ankles together, I hobbled along like a geisha.

The shopping centre was a massive place three floors high, but it was not a comfortable shopping experience because every time I tried to examine something an assistant stood a foot away staring into my face. This was very off-putting even though the assistants were sweet. The shopping centre contained a great supermarket, although I couldn't work out what was in most of the packaged goods. I bought cheese, yoghurt (which may or may not have been Yacoult), and some dragon fruit.

In the pharmacy I finally got through to the ever so patient female assistant that I wanted some aspirin and hoped that is what was in the quaint old-fashioned brown glass bottle she sold me for the equivalent of thirty cents.

Outside again I sloshed and dripped back from whence I came. In the evening I had a visit from a delightful Australian girl, a lawyer who had been working in Laos for a year. We established a connection – she had gone to school with an old friend of mine's daughter.

It was great to be back in Motherland where the service

is remarkable and everyone treats you like family. The waiter told me at dinner that I smelled nice. 'I like your smell,' he said. When I told the staff that I had to leave early in the morning to catch the train, I was written down for a wake-up call and an early breakfast. Unsurprising for a five star hotel, but not usual in guesthouses.

I got up unwillingly at five am to find breakfast ready and waiting. The taxi driver who took me to the station did not abandon me until he had found the platform I needed and handed me over to a porter who delivered me to my train and found my seat (which was a great seat until we moved and it turned into a bucking bronco!)

At first I sat waiting alone in the carriage. Then the vendors found me and came to goggle. Half a dozen of these young people sat themselves around me. One pointed to the scar on my arm and raised her eyebrows in query. It looks strange to others I guess, but now I never think about it nor realise that it is curious to have a zig zag decorating the length of my forearm like the mark of Zorro. I pantomimed cutting and removing an object. Sarcoma and malignancy were beyond this means of communication. Wide-eyed, she absorbed this information and then proceeded to exhibit me, explaining my interesting bits to the others. More vendors of chips and biscuits drifted along to join the fun. When some of them tried to muscle in on me she gently shooed them off. Get your own foreigner, this one is ours.

Unfortunately, no more of my breed showed up to relieve me of the responsibility of providing entertainment for the station's population. I was the sole foreigner on the train. Once again I wondered if there was something I should have gleaned from this.

The carriage was decrepit. The seats, although large and reasonably comfortable, were torn and broken, the linoleum on the floor was stained, grubby and worn through in large patches. Everything that could be was cracked or damaged, walls and windows were stained and beyond help. After a few hours the resident rats summoned the courage to come out to play. They chased each other from one side of the carriage floor to the other. Mind you, these were only small rats. Now I saw how I could have been badly flea bitten on the night train from Mandalay to Thazi on one of my earlier visits. The seats had been fabric but I had wondered how an animal could have got into the train to infest them with fleas. Now I knew. Rats! And rat fleas carry typhus. The only thing I am not vaccinated against – and it's deadly. Surreptitiously I sprayed my seat with repellant.

The train journey began on time and ended only an hour and a half late, taking ten and a half hours, something I was told is perfectly acceptable. We gently edged out of the station with much blowing of the whistle, very necessary in light of the absence of automatic gates at road crossings. We chugged through lots of housing surrounded by piles of rubbish. I am nonplussed by the fact that the Burmese are such clean and beauty-loving people and yet they can live in a house and not notice the mess in the streets around it.

Soon we were in the countryside where everything was lushly green and there was a great deal of water either simply lying about on the ground or in ponds, rivers and canals. We passed over many bridges and stopped for the first time at Bago.

My carriage was called upper class. Finally it was official. I was upper class! My seat was in a row of singles and there were doubles across the aisle. There were few takers for the seats and the empty one in front of me, which was turned to face me, was handy to put my shoeless feet against. I needed this to brace myself. I thought I'd been on rattly, rough rides before but this one this took the grand prize. Not a bit of a jog, trot and lift saddle, this was a full gallop. I had to hang on for dear life and the next day I was stiff and sore and weary from the pummelling I had received. Now and then the noise the train made on the rails made me feel sure that we were about to fall off them – a not uncommon occurrence I had heard. I had been advised not to take the train north right now as that track was especially dangerous in the rainy season.

All this aside, it was a great trip and I got a terrific view of the country from the open windows (they were seized this way). Passing through the villages and towns, I saw horse-drawn carts and more fabulously decrepit WWII army trucks. In the fields there were sleek water buffalo, goats, cows and horses, beige with dark-brown manes and tails, that were more the size of ponies. We jolted and rattled up one side of the Gulf of Martaban and down the other.

After turning to come down the other side there was even more greenery and water with canals, rivers and streams galore. But there were not many people and only a few houses among large tracts of rice. It was easy to see why Burma had once been called the rice bowl of Asia.

The houses were all rattan, thatch and a bit of wood. Most stood with their feet in water. Closer to Moulmein there were villages, one with a mosque with its hammer and sickle moon over the entrance and a Buddhist temple at the other end. Many golden pagodas shone among the greenery.

We stopped at stations about a dozen times. I used the toilet only once. The door would not latch inside. I checked but the one at the other end of the carriage was the same. I wondered why no one had bothered to fix such a simple thing. It was very difficult to hang onto the door to keep it from flying open, as well as to try to brace oneself over a hole in the floor in the rocking and rolling train. I didn't try a second time.

Approaching Moulmein we rattled over an enormously long curving bridge – a pretty amazing piece of work, it was the longest in the country There had been many bridges along the way, crossing areas cut by the countless rivers that ran into the sea. Apart from the Irrawaddy, Burma's two other major rivers are the Chindwin, which runs from Mandalay to the mountains of the north that continue up to the Himalayas, and the Thanlwin here in the east that flows into the Gulf of Martaban. Even the Mekong has a look in, flowing along Burma's border with Laos.

Finally, the journey ended and my bags and I were effortlessly delivered to the Hotel Attran, which is sneered at by backpacker writers as being overpriced. Well, compared to their recommended flop houses maybe it was. I thought it was fabulous. For thirty dollars I got a real hotel. At reception I was presented with a cold towel and a drink, and a plate of grapes followed me to my room.

The rooms of the Attran are bungalows arranged along the river's edge. In front of them were manicured lawns, on which hopped sparrows and birds like ravens, that ran down to end at a low wall beside the water. My room was really a suite, with a sitting room that faced the wide river, a bedroom and a first-class bathroom. There was a flat-screen TV and, perfect for someone like me who is always looking for more light, it had seven lights including a bed light that was like a search beacon.

But I was too pooped even to front for food that night and was in bed by eight o'clock.

chapter 6

Breakfast was served on a deck facing the river in front of reception. I was alone except for two men in one corner and a collection of sparrows and other small birds that saw my entry as a prelude to food. After many attempts, I realised that the waitress was asking if I wanted 'Rice or European'. The 'European' was way beyond her. So she brought a helper who said, 'Eggspotatotoast'. I agreed. I got eggs, a banana (does sound a bit like potato) and virgin toast (toast that has never seen a toaster – white bread naked as the day it was baked). The sparrows were happy to have it. And the coffee was good.

There were a couple of torrential downpours of rain before and after breakfast but the weather fined up for my exploratory walk.

I saw mosques, temples and pagodas and found a riverboat landing, but the boats were only for local use and did not take foreigners as passengers. It was not possible to get a permit to travel anywhere further south from here because of the danger from rebel activity. From the train, now and then I had seen elevated bamboo watchtowers containing a guard surrounded by sandbags, so I presumed there was activity even in this area. The Mon people want independence. Who can blame them?

I thought Moulmein was a much nicer place than Rangoon. I could see why the British had made it their first headquarters in 1827 before making Rangoon their capital in 1885. It was then a major port. Now it has been superseded by Pathein and Yangon, although it still handles a lot of coastal shipping.

For me Moulmein had romantic history. Kipling wrote the *Road to Mandalay* here in the few days that he spent in Burma. (And the road to Mandalay he wrote about was the River Irrawaddy. Hence where the flying fishes play.) This was also where George Orwell lived; it was his family's home for decades.

Dogs were everywhere in the streets. Most did not look in bad nick and some seemed to have owners, although they roamed free. With all the rubbish piled around, they did okay at scavenging.

I was about to hire a trishaw until I saw what the rider was doing. Carefully, daintily, he was extracting lice from his hair and dispatching them between his fingernails. I walked on! I know I couldn't catch lice by sitting behind him in his vehicle, but it put me off. I wandered a long way, passing the extensive frontage of the town markets until I discovered that the next road over ran along the edge of the river. High above the water, shaded by trees, it was a much cooler proposition for strolling.

Most buildings I saw were scruffy and three-storeys high, their narrow walls stained by mould like sooty teardrops running down them. All except the banks, which were fat and glossy palaces. The most substantial and the best maintained looking building I saw was a very large orphanage and school.

Vehicular traffic was mostly motorbike or trishaw. Not all, but some riders wore dark shiny metal helmets shaped like the German army ones of WWII.

Eventually the riverfront road took me back to the Attran after I had passed its next door neighbour, an enormous grand government hotel. I admired its grounds, closely observed by the security guards, but, being a conscientious objector to the government, I could not patronise it.

That day I felt like many people had told me they felt in Laos after long bus rides – that they needed a day to recover. I could not seem to get going. So, this day being Sunday, I declared it a day of rest. Anyway the market was shut on Sunday and there wasn't much more to explore in the town.

I just made it back to my room after lunch before a tremendous downpour swept in. Caught in that, I would have been soaked in seconds. From my windows I could see nothing and even the sound of the TV couldn't be heard above the din on the roof.

The next day I took a non lice-catching driver's trishaw to the Breeze Guest House where I had read bus tickets could be arranged. There I bought a ticket to Bago for four days hence. The bus left at nine am. The train left at an ungodly early hour and anyway I did not think I was up to another train ride just yet. The chirpy old fellow selling me the ticket laughed about the train. 'Like riding a horse,' he said. 'No, an elephant. At a gallop,' I replied.

The trishaw rider then took me on to an eating place – at no stretch of the imagination could it be called a restaurant – situated on the riverbank. I was given such a massive pile of food I could not eat it all so I had it boxed up as takeaway.

Trishaws here were motorbikes with a small – very small – seat attached alongside. They were always an extremely tight fit even for my hips which are generally considered slim. Once a rider had to seize me by both upper arms and haul me out bodily, like extracting a cork from a bottle.

The market was close to the Attran, just a short walk along the street one back from the riverfront which appeared to be the main business area. Where were the shops though? Apart from a couple of tiny places that looked like delis, I saw none and the street was quiet and devoid of pedestrians. The market was a different proposition altogether. It was monstrous and frantically busy and noisy with countless trucks, tuk tuks and bemos picking up and delivering. It backed onto the riverfront and that side of it was also a frenzy of loading and to-ing and fro-ing.

In the evening I tried to get into a bemo taxi – a three-wheeled motorbike with an attached cabin behind it for goods or passengers. You were meant to clamber into the cabin over a back tailgate, but I was wearing my *longii* and, short of hitching it up over my thighs, I couldn't get my leg high enough to get in. I gave up and took a trishaw.

At the Breeze Rest my bus ticket had materialised. I stayed for a while talking to the manager, a kind gentleman who, when I said I wanted some yoghurt, walked me to a shop that sold it. Unfortunately it was sitting in the open in a huge metal vat and looked putrid. We went elsewhere but with no luck. But he did direct me to a place to eat. Called the Help Grandfather and Grandmother Café, it is a charity that supports old people. It was basic but the food I ate there was about the same as anywhere else.

As I left it began to pour and there were no trishaws in sight. I walked, getting wetter and wetter, hobbled by my *longii*, all the way back to the Attran, arriving absolutely soaked. It was dangerous underfoot too. I was likely to slip over on the uneven ground. During the night the rain came down with such noisy ferocity that at times it sounded as though my room would be washed away. The TV had been running constant news of the floods still occurring in Japan and China.

It was still raining in the morning but not as heavily. My breakfast toast had finally been introduced to a toaster, but so far it was only a platonic relationship – no real consummation of the affair had occurred. I was still rattling around in the huge dining room almost alone. There seemed to be few guests beside me.

The tuk tuk I had arranged to take me up to visit the mountain-top temples arrived at ten complete with an Indian driver. There are Karan and Indian people here, hence the mosques. And it was now Ramadan.

We chugged and bounced up high into the hills around the

town, and, stopping at the gates of the first temple complex, Mahamuni Paya, I was put off to walk – minus my shoes – along the slippery tiles, albeit undercover walkways. I was alone apart from a temple guardian or two and a couple of well-cared-for ginger cats.

I came to the shrine of the inner chamber. I had expected this to be small but it was huge with its walls completely covered with little mirrors, while the sides were held up by large mirrored columns. The wall behind the Buddha statue was not only mirrored but set with what were said to be rubies and diamonds. The Buddha was enormous and gilded, partly with real gold. The effect was utterly dazzling.

I walked, careful of the slidy tiles, around the building outside, umbrella aloft. Then we drove further along the ridge to the next temple, Kyaikthanian Paya. It has the area's tallest stupa and a lift that took me to the top, but its electrics failed and I had to inch my way back down, still barefoot, skidding on the damp tiled steps. The view from the parapet had been worth it though. Then it was on to yet more pagodas, everything gold and glittering and accompanied by the tinkling of the little bells that hung from the rooftops.

After a couple of hours we were finished with the Buddhist sites and my driver offered me a church. I could see the cross on its spire in the distance. I declined, opting for lunch instead, and I asked to be taken to the Cinderella Hotel that Mr Anthony from the Breeze Guest House had told me about.

I ate in their restaurant at a table sporting a sign saying 'Europeans only'. Segregated for my sake or theirs? Perhaps my table manners would offend the better class of Burmese. Nevertheless the meal was great and the waiter told me I was beautiful. He lied. I was a frazzled wreck.

chapter 7

Back at my room I found I was locked out. The deadbolt on the door had dropped down on the other side and I couldn't get in. Summoning help, two of the housemaids and I struggled with the recalcitrant lock for a while, then reinforcements in the shape of a workman with a box of tools were called in. We all watched him have no success. Another was summoned and the increasing throng watched him. Two more maids joined us and then the manageress arrived. It was better attended and more entertaining than some stage shows I have been to.

Half an hour later, after trying to break in through the windows and even the roof, another man arrived and simply unscrewed the bolt from its fixings and I was inside! One thing I knew for sure was that no one was going to sneak up on me unawares in the night when I had that bolt on.

The rain then recommenced and continued increasing until the downpour was so torrential I had no hope of getting out to a restaurant or even down to the hotel's dining area. Instead I got out my emergency survival kit and made soup.

The day for my departure came and I left on the nine am bus. In the first village on our journey a woman boarded and the only spare seat was beside a monk. The bus conductor moved a man there and gave the woman his seat. It was unthinkable for a woman to sit next to a monk.

Despite the comfortable ride something still managed to go wrong. I did not arrive where I had intended, Bago. I instead was carried on to Yangon. We had passed through a fairly large town that might have been Bago, but the bus didn't stop and by the time I had thought about it, it was too late. No worries. At the bus station in Yangon I took one of the share taxis that waited there and finally got back to Motherland.

On the way it started again to pour rain. Visibility was almost nil and the streets were flooded a foot deep in rushing torrents. I got drenched going in to ask for a room. I wasn't surprised to be ever so kindly rejected. Motherland was a popular place and I didn't have a booking. I moved on to the Queens Park Hotel where I was received cheerfully even in the drowned rat state I had achieved by then.

Unpacking, I found that water had leaked into my bag and all my clothes were wet. That was the last straw for me with that bag. I had put up with the drunken behaviour of its wonky, wobbly foot and its handle that wouldn't retract without a serious battle, but now it had to go. This wasn't so easy. It refused to leave. After all, it had been with me for years and it wasn't leaving without a struggle. It kept following me around. Twice I put it by the bin downstairs and twice I found it had boomeranged back into my room before I managed to convince the staff that I really didn't want it.

After breakfast the lovely girl at reception rang a bus company for me and arranged a ticket to Taungoo (or two tickets, actually, because I am greedy). They cost eleven dollars. Then I went to the market and bought a suitcase, this time a solid one that wouldn't leak.

The deluge of rain last night had been followed by more this morning and now that it had stopped it was very hot and humid. I went to Motherland for lunch and to book a room for when I came back from my trip north. Then it was on to the shopping centre around the corner. Going around the right corner this time, I found it easily.

On the way back I stopped to admire an enormous tree that stood in the middle of the footpath. It had originally been contained in a massive pot, but had long ago outgrown that and sent its roots out down the sides of the pot and all around it to take over the entire footpath. No one minded this; in fact it had been encouraged to prosper by the addition of two shrines and a spirit house. How could I not love the Burmese? Instead of cutting it back, they worshiped it.

But I don't care for their attitude to waste disposal. The towns I had been to were all unspeakably filthy. Rubbish was just dumped anywhere. Where there was a waterway, garbage was thrown over the edging wall to line the bank several feet from the water, and every now and then rain would wash it down into the river.

Leaving the Queen's Park it was another hour's ride in a taxi to the bus station. It was enormous – the size of a small town. We drove up and down lanes, the driver asking directions now and then, before we reached the bus company office, where I sat down to wait with several other passengers.

I was on my way to Taungoo, north of Yangon on the road that eventually goes to Mandalay, in Burma's flat central area where large amounts of rice are grown. Bago had been temporarily postponed.

It was a great bus and the road we travelled was good, but I was told that it became very bad further north. Although Burma now has fifty two million people, the countryside did not look densely populated. There had been a mere five million at the time the British achieved control of the country, but they had encouraged large numbers of Indian and Chinese migrants.

It took four hours to reach Taungoo and when we arrived I had no problem knowing that I was at the right place. Everyone got off the bus with their baggage so I presumed the ride was over.

As a welcome it immediately began to rain. I hired two trishaws, one for me and one for the bag, and we pedalled off. It then rained some more, and then even more. I got soaked despite my umbrella. The journey felt as though it went on forever – down the long main road that led out of town, off onto a rutted water-logged mud track, and finally along a tiny rustic tree-shaded lane, at the end of which I came to a well-hidden little gem – the Beauty Rest Guesthouse.

I felt guilty about having made the poor trishaw riders pedal so far and in the rain too, so when they asked for three thousand for the pair of them, I gave them six. This horrified the guesthouse staff who had come out to welcome me. They protested at such profligate behaviour, but I said, 'No. It was a long way. And in the rain.' (And three thousand is two dollars fifty!)

I was shown into a room that looked like paradise. It was dry! A smiling woman brought me a bottle of water and two plates of fruit and I set about drying out. My room was one of two upstairs in a pavilion made entirely of wood. It was big with many windows and a multitude of lights and electric plugs, not all of which worked of course and not until after six in the evening.

The lights were a real thrill but the wide balcony was the best feature of this accommodation. It encompassed a wonderful, all-green outlook – large expanses of rice fields that stretched to a dense line of dark-green trees. A village hid in there behind those trees from which, across the rice fields in the early morning and late evening, came the chant of the monks in its monastery.

What a blissful place to spend a few days.

My room, although exceedingly comfortable, looked like the house that Jack built. A bit Bush Carpenter constructed, it was made entirely of wood – floors, walls and furniture. The floor was a beautiful parquet of several woods. The walls were polished mahogany, gleaming and shining; even the ceiling was wood. And the furniture! A whole antique shop crammed in, jostling each other for space – massive, heavily carved and oppressively overbearing stuff that weighed a ton. There was a glass-topped coffee table as big as a bed and a wardrobe with an aged and foxed-mirrored door with a magnificent glass handle that unfortunately didn't serve its purpose because the door didn't open. Neither did the drawers of the elaborate dressing table as half of it was jammed behind the bed. Lumped wherever possible onto any flat surface were clunky carved wooden ornaments, and on the floor, standing sentry duty beside the bathroom door, was a huge wooden rhinoceros. A rhinoceros?

The rear window was behind the wardrobe. I had to squeeze in to open the curtains. There were more windows around the room and the wide front one had a wonderful outlook over the balcony to the rice paddies.

The rice was in various stages of growth and the villagers came a few at a time to work in the fields, some planting rice shoots and one ploughing with an ox. They all went home when it began to rain heavily, leaving the ox standing alone in the downpour. I was happy when he was finally collected and taken away, hopefully to a nice dry stable, leaving the paddy to the egrets who stalked regally among the plants.

Below the balcony a profusion of palms and trees grew luxuriantly and the fields came up to within a metre of them. The noise of the frogs at night was deafening. Added to the delights of this place, I found a resident dog and cat to talk to, as well as the charming man who was the owner, a doctor who ran a clinic in the town.

In the mornings a sensational breakfast was laid out on a communal table groaning under the weight of platters of tropical fruit and other life-sustaining goodies. Lunch and dinner were ordered in advance and also eaten communally in the ground floor, net-enclosed dining room that doubled as the reception area. I met a couple of German women teachers there who were good company at dinner each night when we shared large bottles of beer.

Much as I didn't want to leave this idyllic place, I enquired about onward travel and learned that the train south to Bago left at eleven am. That beat the bus that departed in the middle of the night well six am actually. Yes, I was about to try once more to go to Bago.

A trishaw to transport me to the train station was conjured up. It was a long ride to the station for the trishaw rider, but this time at least it was not raining. At the entrance a guard took control of me and led me to the station master's office, where we went through the passport and US dollar ritual again. It took a lot of writing of papers and filling in of forms before a ticket was allowed into my possession, costing ten dollars. I was taken to a seat, far away at the end of the platform, to wait.

The train arrived almost on time and I found my seat, a single similar to the one I'd had on the Moulmein train. The carriage was grotty but quite comfortable. Before we left the station master came aboard to seek me out and enquire if I was happy with my situation.

The ride to Bago was rough but nowhere as rough as my previous train trip. The windows were too filthy to see through, so it was a good thing that they had solidified in the half-open position and I could see over the top. There were few passengers in this upper class carriage, but a profusion of vendors passed through intermittently hawking chips, lollies and unidentifiable objects in mysterious bags.

Although the bus takes two hours to Bago, this train ride took six. We stopped for ages on an elevated bridge in the middle of rice paddies with nothing in sight, probably due to a breakdown. This train thankfully had a lockable toilet, but it was still a major acrobatic feat to use it as I had to cling desperately to a pipe on the wall with one hand.

We arrived at Bago station only two hours late, which I believe is par for the course. On the platform I was kidnapped by a smooth type, who shunted me into a trishaw and in light rain sent me off to inspect a hotel he recommended, despite my saying that I wanted to go to the Bago Star Hotel. He followed behind on a motorbike, no doubt in order to squeeze a commission out of the hotel for obtaining my body. The place we arrived at looked a frightful tip and I did not even go in for an inspection. Agreeing to look at another that turned out to be miles away, I was pedalled off in the rain feeling terribly guilty about the poor man pushing me along.

The town was semi-flooded and the trishaw man had to wade, shoving me through foot-high lakes across streets. I offered to walk up the hills we came to but he said, 'No', and got off to push the bike with much panting and wheezing on what were by then dirt tracks. We had left the town after crossing a high bridge over the Bago River and turned off onto a rutted strip of bitumen that led onto dirt and rubble paths. Still we continued on, until finally we pulled into the courtyard of a building. By this time I would have said yes to any old dump to end the rider's, and my, torment, but happily the place he had brought me to was lovely.

Its name, Shwe See Seim, translates as The Three Seasons. First I was shown a downstairs room and told it was thirteen dollars. Next, a bungalow that looked like – of all unlikely things – a Swiss chalet. This was seventeen dollars. Still further we continued in the tour of the place till the *pièce de résistance* was produced. Upstairs with a little Juliet balcony, was a large comfortable room that cost twenty dollars. I asked about electricity and was told, 'Yes. Is electric. Not every, but some'. This I took to mean that it came and went at will. Bless it.

To prove a point, the lights went out the minute I attempted to enter the room. It was bucketing down rain by then. We were in the middle of a big storm. My escort explained that the electricity's excuse this time was that a tree had fallen down. He gave me a suspiciously at-hand torch.

After a quick wash I went in search of food. Downstairs behind the guesthouse was a large dining room with a limited menu written only in Burmese. But I was starving and indicated that I would eat anything on offer. What did come tasted rather good even though I had no idea what it was.

I was stumbling around getting ready for bed by torchlight when the lights blared on. What a shock. This place in the sticks had the best and the most lights of anywhere I had stayed in so far – eight in all and only one not working. It was as dim as all get out in the bathroom though so it was morning before I got the full impact of it. By daylight it was a shock to the senses. There was a whacking great bathtub big enough to wash an elephant in painted in an overpowering bright royal blue, as were all the other fittings – a shocking symphony in electrifying blue. I used the shower; that bath was far too intimidating.

After the included and adequate breakfast early the next morning I stood on my little balcony and watched the veggies being delivered. The seller arrived, a woman with a wide, flat basket of goodies on her head. The cook joined her and they both squatted on their haunches to discuss and decide.

Despite its difficult-to-access position, or because of it, it was lovely here. As soon as you left the main road the surroundings became rural and rustic, shaded paths among a plethora of greenery. I went for a walk around the small dirt lanes. Not far away was a monastery. Now that we were halfway into Buddhist lent I noticed that more frequent chanting came from the monasteries. Soon it would be the full moon of Waso when the big festival of the Buddhist Rains Retreat is held.

The only drawback to this idyllic place was that it was not near any transport. I wasn't going to subject a trishaw rider to another of those gruelling journeys out here, so transport had to be called for by the hotel staff. Due to a communication problem, the tuk tuk I requested turned out to be my friend and his motorbike again.

I wanted to visit the Golden Rock and had tried unsuccessfully to negotiate a ride there through the hotel. Friend took me, an unwilling pillion passenger on his motorbike, to the taxi drivers in the town. This was a failed enterprise as they all said that they couldn't go up there in the current weather.

The Golden Rock, Mount Kyaiktiyo, one of Burma's holiest Buddhist sites, is a huge gold-plastered boulder precariously balanced on a mountain top. Legend says that a precisely placed hair of the Buddha in the stupa on top of it maintains its balance and that the boulder was found at the bottom of the sea. This holy shrine attracts countless pilgrims who laboriously climb the arduous path to the top where only men are allowed to cross the bridge over the chasm in front of the rock and place gold leaf on it.

By now Bago township was flooded. The streets were awash and in some parts, narrow, flat-bottomed canoes were being used to navigate along them. Motorbikes were getting stuck and people were wet to the knees.

I had a real coffee finally, found for me by my friend whom by now I could not get rid of. But he was interesting to talk to and he did speak English well. I think he was of Indian extraction. I gave him some money and he took me back to my guesthouse, returning in the evening with a young couple who had a tuk tuk so that I could arrange a jaunt for the next day with them. I had baulked at more motorbike riding.

chapter **8**

The young couple and their tuk tuk turned up at nine in the morning and we set off. Heading through the town streets that were rivers of swirling, muddy water, we were soon on the road out to the pagodas and shrines. Really only tracks, the roads were appalling all mud and rubble.

There were horses, buffalo, pigs and goats in the villages and the fields around them. All the animals looked well fed which was not surprising with the lush green feed that abounded, and the rubbish that they had to fossick in. But the dogs worried me. There were far too many dogs wandering everywhere – the streets, shops, temples and pagodas.

In the proceeding time I did four hours hard labour, for which privilege I paid my escort twenty dollars. I told them that they should have paid me – I did all the work while they sat and waited in comfort.

But the sites were stupendous. The former capital of several past kingdoms, Bago has more fabulous temples than anywhere else in Burma, as well as the enormous Kha Khat Wain Kyaung Monastery, the third biggest in the country. Previously called Pegu, Bago was a thriving port on the Pegu River before the river changed its course and cut the town off from the sea.

Our first call was the Shwethalyaung Buddha, a reclining statue 180 feet long and 53 feet high. Its original date is uncertain but it was already considered old in 1769 when records tell of it being restored after an earthquake. I stood before it, dwarfed by the mind-boggling size of it. Just its little finger measured ten feet. That's some digit.

Gold- and mirror-decorated pillars marched the length of the hall that housed the Buddha. Walls, also patterned with mirrors and gold, surrounded it. The statue was currently being washed. Men diminished by its size to ants crawled on it wielding long handled brooms.

My escort and I moved on, jolting and crashing in and out of potholes, to another reclining Buddha. This one was outdoors. Sprawling is a more apt description than reclining; the Naung Daw Gyi Mya Tha Lyaung is 250 feet long.

Several more sites followed including, towering over all, the glittering 376 foot high Shwemawdaw Stupa – 46 feet higher than the Shwe Dagon in Yangon.

My escort team was a lovely young couple, newly married and trying to make enough money for a house. They took it upon themselves to become my minders, which was endearing, although they did rather treat me as though I was in my dotage. Every now and then the sweet young girl would lean over into the back of the tuk tuk, where I sat in the tiny open cabin, and gently fan me. And if I was too long in a temple she would come looking for me, thinking perhaps that I had succumbed to the strain.

Then we found the snake! Enthroned in splendour in its own pagoda, the Snake Monastery, lives a gigantic Burmese python. It is believed to be the reincarnation of an especially holy monk and is 127 years old. About seventeen feet long – who would be game to stretch it out to measure it – one foot wide and very thick, it looked exceeding solid and heavy as it lay with its beautifully patterned brown, beige and black body coiled in graceful, sinuous loops along a carpeted dais.

This venerated and worshipped reptile – sorry, monk – scoffs down eleven pounds of chicken every ten days and is possibly the world's biggest living snake. I did see a longer anaconda in Brazil but it was stuffed (in every sense of the word) and much thinner. This boy looked heavy. It was fascinatingly beautiful, but it still seemed sinister to me.

Donations of money from adoring fans lay all along its sleek body and its own personal servant sat cross-legged beside it, attending its every need. Nearby was a tiled pool for its bath and woollen rugs to keep it warm at night. What a life – although it could have got a bit boring. Deciding that it would be a good idea to placate this awesome creature, I lay a few kyat notes beside it and stroked it cautiously. It remained immobile and didn't seem to mind. I guess at 127 years of age you wouldn't have the energy to get up and chase a tourist.

At dinner in the Three Seasons someone else finally appeared in the dining room that up until now I'd had sole use of. It was a convention of men who after a while produced a microphone and some absolutely appalling and very loud singing. I bolted through my dinner and left.

Early the following morning I was ready to move back to Yangon. I had found that the cost of a long distance taxi was reasonable and it beat the difficult bus times. The hotel manager rang the number I had been given to ask the driver to collect me, but Friend and his motorbike turned up instead. He said the taxi driver wanted another five thousand kyat. He could not look me in the eye when he said this so I knew it was a con. He also entered my room, shut the door and lay on my bed to deliver the message, which is not done in polite circles, Burma or anywhere. I paid him the five thousand to get rid of him.

It was a good, if fast, ride to Yangon for the twenty-six dollars it cost me. I found the behaviour of the people along the narrow road amazing. They gave no heed whatever to traffic and finally I realised why. Their attitude was that it is not for them to look out for vehicles, but it is the vehicles responsibility to avoid them. They wander, stand or even sit on the road, as do the dogs, who have obviously taken their cue from them. I saw up to six dogs together at a time just standing in the middle of the road. Like the rubbish thrown everywhere, they didn't seem to be seen as a problem.

In Yangon once, only once, I saw a rubbish collector. He wore heavy gloves and a mask as he wielded a witch's broom to sweep litter up and shovel it into a wooden push cart. Then he probably dumped it somewhere, possibly in the river.

I received a great welcome at Motherland, like a long lost relative returning. This time my room was a floor higher and I had a treetop outside the window and a view of the bush-enshrouded train line below.

Next day I set off to see the gem museum. Wow! There is some amazing loot in there. It is housed in an enormous squeaky clean place, a marked contrast to the grot of the streets outside. Loads of attendants stood about and two guards at a desk outside made me cough up five dollars and my passport, the details of which were copied.

On the ground and first floors were countless stalls and shops selling gems, jade and jewellery. I bought some jade, I hoped. But I hoped in vain. By the time my sister the gemologist tested it, it had metamorphosed into dyed quartz. It was super cheap if that's a consolation.

The top floor contained the museum collection that was understandably not for sale. There were stupendously valuable and beautiful articles encased here, giving a glimpse of the fabulous riches this country has had in the past. There was the world's largest sapphire found north of Mandalay, a mere trinket of 63,000 carats, also the largest jade boulder, rough ruby and star sapphire. But what I would have taken home if it had not been under the eagle eye of a guard, was a foot-high apple-green jade elephant caparisoned with gold and jewel-bedecked howdah and trimmings.

I headed across town in a taxi then to have lunch at the Strand hotel. I couldn't leave Burma without revisiting this icon of old Rangoon. But I was fearful that my pleasant memories were in for disillusionment. The riverfront Strand Road is still lined with many of the wonderful colonial buildings remaining from British days. Some are in good condition, but some, like many others in the town, are spacious buildings in extensive grounds and look forlorn and seem to have been left to rot.

Happily I saw that the Strand exterior was unchanged, albeit much cleaner and smarter than when last I had approached it. Although the hotel façade remained the same, inside I did not recognise it. It had been mightily restored and was very grand indeed. It now cost hundreds of dollars a night as opposed to the ten that it had cost for a double room when I stayed there on my first visit to Burma years ago. And where was the well-remembered long wooden bar where we had sat and conned our way into the use of kyats instead of dollars? The Strand Hotel and its wonderful old bar were one of my lasting memories of my first visit to Burma. Where the bar had been was now an arcade of super expensive shops. But then on one side of the foyer, I entered a room and there, running its length, was a long wooden bar. I like to believe that it is the original.

I saved revisiting the Shwedagon Pagoda for my final day. As the Strand is the symbol of British Burma, the Shwedagon is the symbol of its Buddhist magnificence. It was just as incredible as I remembered. Surely one of the wonders of the world, I could see its great glittering golden dome reaching heavenwards from far away. Slowly I climbed the hundreds of steps and stairways that bring you up to the extensive complex around the base from where the stupa rises – an awesome great lump of gold, 322 feet to the point of the *psi* on its top that contains an enormous diamond.

Legend says that the Shwedagon is thousands of years old but archeologists date the original stupa as sixth century. That still makes it 1600 years old, which is a fair age in anybody's book. It is said to have been built around a relic of the

Buddha – though if all those teeth and hairs were really his he must have had more than the usual allotment of follicular and dental equipment. A toothy hairy person, albeit most holy.

I glided barefoot, in the company of people quietly praying and making offerings around the base of the stupa, on cool paved courtyards worn smooth by the constant tread of worshipping feet. Surrounding the base, nestled into its sides, are many small pagodas, stupas and shrines, all gilded. Untold glittering gold, more than all the gold contained in the vaults of the Bank of England, cover the sides of the Shwedagon, as well as diamonds, rubies and emeralds.

Inscriptions on the eastern stairway record that Queen Shinsawbu began the gilding craze in the 15th century when she plastered the stupa with her weight (eighty eight pounds), in gold. Then her son-in-law, in a feat of unsurpassed one-upmanship, applied four times his and his wife's weight.

chapter 9

It was not hard to leave Burma but it was sad. I wanted to stay longer but my allocated twenty-eight days were up and I had to go. I arrived prematurely early at the airport, determined to have plenty of time to deal with any contingencies. I did not trust this airport; it held stressful memories.

In Singapore I asked the woman at the Tourist Accommodation desk to find me a room for the night. I planned to go on to Kuala Lumpur in the morning. I did not want to go back to the Australian winter just yet and Malaysia was a country I had travelled through several times but had never stopped in long enough to discover. She found me a hotel, but told me that it was in Geylang, the red light district, and I should not go out at night! As if anyone was going to accost me with all the talent likely to be about. When I told her that I was going on to Kuala Lumpur, she said that she had been 'snatched' there. She meant her bag, not her, I think.

The airport shuttle took me to the hotel. Walking around the corner from it (in the daylight, just in case), I found a small restaurant where I had a meal. The next morning I boarded a bus to KL.

The bus was almost empty, with just four of us in a double-deckered deluxe vehicle that came with a personal video screen, an audio player and lunch delivered on a tray. Plantations of oil palms lined almost the entire route to KL, a depressing sight and testimony that the native rainforest and food farmland had been obliterated. Oil palms are extremely detrimental to the environment. Few towns or villages were visible from the elevated highway we rode along and we passed through none. We made one loo stop. I am like the Queen, of whom it is said never passes up the chance for a toilet break.

In KL I took a taxi to the Grocer's Inn, the guesthouse in Chinatown where I had made a booking. It had been highly recommended by the guide book writers, who said that it was 'old and interesting'. It was old for sure. It was also a dump. That's the last time I trust them. Have I said this before?

I took the most expensive room in the Grocer's Inn – they said it had a bathroom. They forgot to mention that the bathroom had no hot water or anything much else for that matter. The room was horrible, the solitary light was dismal – and there was no window! It was like being entombed. There was just a bed and a broken old dressing table, the drawers of which contained the detritus of the last hundred or so inmates. With no space to put anything on the floor, I had to sleep with my bag on the other half of the bed.

I got out of this squalid flophouse as fast as I could, largely unwashed, the next morning. The previous evening I had scouted the street for better digs. Chinatown has many small hotels, some of which are brothels. I enquired at one that didn't appear to be one of those, and it was such a relief to find something decent so I grabbed it. It cost only four dollars more than the dingy hovel I was currently in, where they had even made me pay an extra dollar for a towel. And forget the soap. They certainly had.

I moved my bag across the street and into the Hotel Yeang Ying. This street was Jalan Sultan, which intersects Jalan Petaling, the night market street. It was an interesting place to stay even though the taxi driver, an Indian, had warned me, 'It's full of Chinese. Do not to go out at night'. Funny that Chinatown is full of Chinese and it's not a good idea to go to a night market – at night!

I found a cafe two doors from the hotel for breakfast and in front of it I saw a stop for the Ho Ho – a hop on, hop off tourist bus. I bought a ticket and hopped on. A twenty-four hour ticket only cost twelve dollars Australian. The bus took a long time to go around its twenty-three stops so it was a good way to observe the town and its life.

After Burma, Malaysia was strikingly clean. And another blessing was that there were no dogs, although I did see the odd cat. I read a letter to the paper from an Asian tourist in which he complained that he had seen two dogs shot in the street by police and then dragged away, leaving blood and mess in their wake. Muslims generally don't like dogs and consider them, like pigs, an unclean animal.

KL is full of beautiful old buildings, mosques and markets, but it only dates from 1857 when a town grew up from what was originally a tin miners' camp. The British established themselves here in the 19th century but the Japanese invasion during WWII ended British occupation. By 1963 independence had been achieved and Kuala Lumpur became the capital of what was to become Malaysia.

The bus slowly drove past the famous PETRONAS Twin Towers that Malaysians are inordinately proud of – the reason for which eluded me. I thought they were hideous. Malevolent-looking, grey, shiny metal fingers, they point straight up in the air for a great distance without anything to relieve their sombreness. These utilitarian steel-clad monsters were completed in 1998 and are eighty-eight storeys and 452 metres high, making them the seventh highest structure in the world. A bridge connects the two towers about halfway up at an enormous height and I was told that for a fee I could walk across it. No fear. You'd have to pay *me* – heaps – and you'd still need a cattle prod to force me out onto there. But I loved Merdeka (Freedom) Square. Ringed by magnificent heritage buildings, it is one of the most spectacular squares I have seen anywhere.

Almost the full bus circuit later I got off at the Bintang

(Star) Walk where all the up-market shops like Lacroix and Louis Vuitton are, not that they were my aim. I was looking for Lowyat Plaza where computers are sold. Recently my little portable had begun a slow progression toward what I feared might be eventual extinction. It was refusing to register d's, which made for some very interesting words, and I also need two d's to get into my email. After going from counter to counter and floor to floor – all ten of them – I decided not to buy another computer. Gone are the days of electronic bargains in this part of the world.

My second afternoon in KL was also spent on the Ho Ho bus. I had tried to get a taxi at midday but no one would take me across town at this time because the traffic builds up horrendously then. Instead I got on the bus and got off at the bird park. What a terrific place. A few of the birds, the predators who cannot be trusted not to eat the other inmates, are in large enclosures. The rest fly or stalk, in the case of the flamingos, free, clearly visible and unafraid of humans under the high overhead netting that covers the entire eight hectares of the park. I entered the enclosure through a set of double mesh doors that allowed me in but not the birds out. The first long walkway contains large parrots of various colours, many perching on branches right in front of me. There are two hundred species of birds here, including hornbills and eagles, among trees and ponds and natural forest. I enjoyed this park immensely and spent hours there.

Not far from Chinatown was my favourite building. Not surprisingly for a train lover, it was the KL Train Station. Built in 1911 in a Moorish design, it is a glorious confection of white-painted turrets and towers. Not a bit like what you would expect a functional place like a train station would be, it is a cross between an Arabian night's fantasy palace and a mosque. Originally Butterworth and Singapore trains came here, now they go to the newer Sentral Station; but on my first two journeys through Malaysia my train had stopped here.

I remained in KL for a week and enjoyed all of it except for the horrible pollution that coloured everything greyish and the traffic that made it difficult to get about. The hotel staff was kind and helpful. Taxis were cheap, although they rarely had meters and the cost increased due to the roundabout way you had to go in the one-way traffic system. But almost all the drivers were friendly and most gave me a discount if the fare went over the round dollar fee.

Another difficulty I found was that it was Ramadan, the Muslim month of fasting, when many services are cut back or not available, so information about onward travel was hard to come by. I visited the lovely restored mansion that is now the Tourist Bureau and even there had no luck. But eventually I happened upon a local train station close to Jalan Sultan that sold long distance bus tickets. I bought one to Malacca, an old and interesting port on the Malay Peninsula beside the Straits of Malacca.

The bus took two hours to travel the 148 kilometres south-east to reach its terminus in the Malacca bus station – an enormous, busy place, some distance from the town centre. Bus was evidently the way to travel here – there were great numbers of them, well organised into local, intercity and international areas. There were also many shops and stalls as well as a money changer.

I had booked a room in Malacca at the Best Western Riverside Hotel. It was well positioned close to the centre and my room looked into the Malacca River as promised. I repaired the toilet system in my capacity of Travelling Plumber, then took a taxi to the centre of the tourist drag, the Stadthuys (red house), a large red building that is a relic of Malacca's days as a Dutch trading port.

Originally a fishing village and later a Malay sultanate, as well as the domain of sea people who specialised in piracy, Malacca sits at a strategic position on the narrowest part of the Strait that forms a passage from China to India. For aeons it had been a stopping place for ships, including the fleet of Zheng Ho, the famous Ming dynasty admiral of the 13th century. Taken over by the Portuguese in 1511, the port was wrested from them by the Dutch in 1641 who in turn ceded it to Britain in 1826. The British left in 1946 and eventually Malacca became part of Malaysia.

In the square surrounding the Stadthuys I got on what I thought was another hop on, hop off bus. This was a fair assumption, as I had been standing under a sign for it. However, this was not the Ho Ho. This bus travelled a long, long route, and finally expelled me back again in the already familiar central bus station that I had left not two hours before.

The bus had been very crowded and I'd had to stand all the way packed closely in a bunch of eight delightful young Italians from Naples. In the hour we spent together we became friends and when we got off the girls all kissed me and promised to email. A long wait later another bus took me back from whence I came. I asked the driver to let me off at the street I thought led to my hotel on the river and, amazingly, it did.

Next day I bought a ticket for a jaunt on the river. The riverboat stopped at a landing right outside the hotel to collect me. Many tourist boats cruise up and down the Malacca River, which flows through the town and is its main feature. The riverside is wonderful. The heart of the old city, it is intersected by curved bridges and lined with tiny, brightly painted, two-storey 300-year-old houses standing shoulder to shoulder.

At first I had the boat almost to myself, then I was swamped by a mob of riotous Chinese who frolicked on board like children, singing, laughing and photographing everything in sight, especially me the peculiar-looking foreigner. I must be in every photo that went home to China.

Finally I got off at the hotel landing where I had started and walked back along the river to the centre of town. How nice this walk was, along an immaculately kept paved path beside the water, shaded by the densely packed little houses and edged by lovingly tended pot plants. This very old part of Malacca is now UNESCO World Heritage listed. Along the way were many boat landings where I saw signs advertising a hop on, hop off boat, but, Ramadan again, no one could tell me about it. I found the Tourist Bureau but they were useless, and the supposed boat ticket office was closed except for a man sleeping (the guard!) outside it on a bench. There were few individual travellers here and only tour groups seemed to be catered for.

I sat down on one of the many seats overlooking the river for a rest and was immediately engulfed by more jolly Chinese and photographed some more – once with a woman tenderly entwined about me. This must be the new Chinese middle class. God help us when they can all afford to travel. All 1.2 billion of them! They either weren't allowed out before or couldn't afford it.

Although Malacca wasn't as hot as KL, said to be the hottest place in the country where the temperature can reach 40°C, I got tired walking about after a while so I retreated until the evening. It was pleasant then to amble along Yongers Street, Malacca's famous Chinese night market.

The following day I took a Duck Tour. The duck wasn't Donald but an amphibious vehicle. This was fun. A group of Chinese (more photographs) tourists and I sat high on the open top of the duck under an awning as we chugged around town passing the sights. We saw the Malacca Tower, another great pointy article that I was urged to climb but again resisted, refusing to be a Good Little Tourist. This tower was not only sickeningly high, but, to make matters worse, it revolved!

Then our duck drove down a causeway and straight into the sea, which was a great novelty. On the nearby headland, sailing now, we passed a spectacular mosque, the Straits of

Malacca Mosque, that guards the land and the sea it looks out over. We chugged along the waters of the coast a way and then returned.

I had lunch at a small cafe on the river's edge where very good food and a banana split all cost a mere four dollars. Waving down a riverboat, I got on wanting to go one stop but instead spent an hour trying to get off it again. When I finally managed this I walked back to the Best Western Riverside through a profusion of small, interesting backstreets. Stopping at a local market, I bought fruit and other essential supplies. Then I called an end to the day's explorations.

I tried to book another couple of nights in the hotel but could only get one as everything was full. The coming weekend was the beginning of the four-day celebration of the end of Ramadan, Ide el Fittr, which I was familiar with from my Saudi days. I used the hotel's wifi to try to find somewhere to stay. It was hopeless. Everywhere was full.

Dinner time came and I walked to where I had seen a few restaurants and nearby noticed the Accordion Hotel. It looked okay so I convinced the woman presiding over the desk to accommodate me when I had to leave the Riverside. She had said no at first, then relented, having perhaps concluded that, although decidedly strange, I was not actually dangerous. I paid a deposit and ate dinner on the opposite corner at a Chinese restaurant. I had rice balls and chicken, a local specialty, and it was the best, most perfectly cooked chicken I have ever had. It was accompanied by some chicken soup that tasted as though the chicken had merely walked through the bowl of water (without washing its feet), and a battered tin mug of what the waiter alleged was tea, but I doubt it. It was a strange, thick, dark-orange brew with scum on the top. I gave that a miss.

I returned to my room at the Riverside happy, securely accommodated and well fed. In two days I moved to the Accordion. Checking out, to my surprise I was given a thirty-seven ringgit (currently about three to a dollar) refund. I have no idea why. I must have been unknowingly a Good Little Tourist.

The Accordion was on a corner of one of the main streets that lead down to the town centre and the Red House. From my front room I had a good view of the street action but at first I felt I was on the *Marie Celeste*. I saw no other guests even when I sat in the lobby. Then the holidays came and the guests flooded in, and the usually empty downstairs area was full of prams and baby seats and families with children.

Coffee was provided in the downstairs area and I sat there sometimes to talk to the staff. I couldn't find anyone else who spoke English. Under interrogation the manager told me that he had spent four years in Perth – in Maylands, the suburb next to the one I had lived in there, Victoria Park. And one of the women receptionists had a daughter at school in Adelaide, the Islamic school two streets from where I live.

I taxied to Maketta Parade, a massive shopping complex. Getting about by taxi was often circuitous and convoluted due to the pesky one-way road system that operated here, as it did in KL, and the heavy traffic. In Makatta Parade I found a bookshop. I desperately needed something to read. From a line of cheap re-printed classics on the English shelf I selected *The Moonstone* by Wilkie Collins, a book I had always meant to read.

Outside there was a long queue for taxis. I sat on a bench for twenty minutes talking to an old man while I waited. After a while something started to click and I was about to ask him if I had met him before. Then a taxi came and it was my turn to leave. It was only in the taxi that I remembered who he was. He was the kind, elderly gentleman I had met travelling on the train through Malaysia when I was on my way to Laos who had shared his tea with me. Yet another of those strange chance meetings that happen when travelling. But what a lost opportunity. He would have been delighted that he had been mentioned in my previous book, *Lost in Laos*.

On the day that the holidays officially started, a massive red banner was hung across the street under my window – Selamat Hari Raya. In the evening I watched the police cordoning off the street to control the traffic to the night market. Apparently everyone goes to Yonkers on this night.

Two days later I took a bus to Singapore where I had a date with Qantas. Getting off at Johor Bahru on the end of the Malaysian peninsular, I taxied to the airport and went home.

chapter **10**

Ten months later I was on my way back to Burma for the fifth time. This time I left Adelaide on a ship, my preferred method of travel, but it was not going to Burma. In fact, I was setting off in completely the opposite direction, but that's nothing new for me. I was about to sail halfway around Australia and almost all of the way around New Zealand to reach Singapore from where I could get to Burma.

The freighter *Buxstar* arrived at Outer Harbour on time. At the container terminal gate the guard greeted me by my first name. He had been expecting me, the only passenger boarding here. My date with the immigration and customs officers who came to clear me went swimmingly despite the embarrassment my bag full of pills and lotions always causes me. I look like a travelling chemist shop.

I checked in with the security watchman at the top of the *Buxstar*'s gangplank, signed on in the ship's office and, hey presto, I was officially a seafarer. Hauling my bags up the stairway to the cabins, the officer of the deck asked if I wanted the owner's cabin. Of course I did! It is big and would have cost me fifteen euros more a day if I'd had to pay for it.

The *Buxstar* is a huge German-built ship of 40,000 tons that was carrying 3700 containers (not fully loaded). Although she belongs to a German company, she is registered in Monrovia and sails under a Liberian flag. My accommodation consisted of a spacious day cabin, a small bedroom and a bathroom. It had masses of storage, a fridge and a TV and DVD. One porthole had an excellent view of the lifeboat, reassuringly close in case of Abandon Ship calls. The other two were occluded by containers.

I met the Filipino captain who introduced me to the cook, also Filipino. Hooray, this augured well for the food. The second officer was appointed my custodian. Another Filipino, as were all the crew, he was a fine, big, handsome fellow with a devastating smile that never seemed to leave his face as he gave me the ship's safety tour despite the Disaster areas, lifeboats and distress signals that featured heavily in this adventure. There were the Man Overboard Rules – Throw Life Ring. Call for help. Launch open life-raft. (Calling I could do okay, scream, in fact, but I wasn't sure about the others). But he said that when the Abandon Ship call came, one of the crew would come to escort me to the lifeboat. Not if, *when*! Nice.

A trapdoor above the porthole in my cabin was pointed out to me. It was marked by a sign – 'Life Line' – and surrounded by a fluorescent strip so it could be found during light failures or dense smoke. It was a wonder I didn't get off immediately after contemplating all the nasty things that could happen to me on this ship, but the Life Line was the worst. Its trapdoor opened to reveal a rope with which I was expected to attach myself, then jump out of the porthole and over the side of the ship. No thanks. I would look like bait on the end of a fishing line to a passing shark!

We left sometime during the night and I woke to a gentle swell and a grey, cold day. The young Filipino steward came wanting to clean my cabin but I fended him off. Give me time to mess it up first. It was his first ship and I was the first female passenger he had had to deal with. He was justifiably terrified of me.

Two days later we were sailing up the Yarra River to our berth in Port Melbourne. The Stella Maris van took me to the Seaman's club in Little Collins Street – all part of the wonderful service they provide to seafarers, a definition that includes anyone travelling on a working ship. On the bus I met some Indians who were on shore leave from a ship carrying dangerous chemicals. I was glad to hear they were anchored far away from us. The berths next to us were occupied by CMA CGM's *Manet*, sister ship of the *La Tour* and *Matisse* on which I have travelled, and the *Italia*.

Returning from shore leave, I climbed the *Buxstar*'s very high and wobbly gangplank hanging onto the dirty, oily rope sides. At the top my hands were seized by the seaman on security watch and scrubbed with a cloth. I was polished up like a grubby three year old and given a pair of workman's gloves for future use.

The crew of the *Buxstar* from the captain down were a cheerful lot, always smiling and laughing. All except the Ukrainian chief engineer were Filipino. There was one other passenger on the ship when I boarded, Dave, a New Zealander, and we collected another here in Melbourne, Rick from the UK, who was on a quest to go around the world in eighty days without flying.

Two days later we arrived in Botany Bay, the container port for Sydney. I went to the gate with the wharf van and waited in a shed with some of the crew and the captain for the mission to Seafarers Flying Angel van that took us to the city. It was a lovely sunny day, everything was bright and green after heavy rain the previous night. The bus took a scenic route past the iconic Harbour Bridge and Opera House. The Seafarers had moved since I was here last and is now almost on the waterfront.

Back at the ship I was a good little passenger and used the gloves I had been given, and this time didn't need cleaning up by the crew. In the morning I saw, to my delight, that the containers that had blocked the outlook from two of my portholes were gone. I could see right to the mast and the front of the ship. Now to get rid of the lifeboat. Or maybe not.

I stood on the deck as we sailed through the heads of Botany Bay, watching planes taking off from Mascot Airport alongside us. The captain told me that there was now a serious low out in the Tasman Sea and we would be taking a different route further south towards Antarctica to try to avoid it.

The swell began in the afternoon and by evening it was extreme. We started to roll badly. We did not have enough weight to hold us steady – many of our containers had already been discharged and some of the remainder were empty. Everything bounced about my cabin; nothing would stay on shelves or surfaces. It was very difficult to move around. During the night I was actually afraid for the first time on a ship. I felt we were about to tip over. In bed I had having visions of being called to the lifeboat. I lay in the dark deciding what to take with me – passport, money, lipstick … yes, lipstick, a girl can't face a lifeboat full of sailors without lipstick.

All that day and the next it remained very rough. The captain spent the entire time on the bridge; he even slept there. And he kept the crew working at inside jobs. It was too dangerous out on deck. Later I heard that this storm had been the severest in this area for years and that roofs had been blown off houses in Wellington in two hundred mile per hour winds. And that, yes, a ship had once overturned in such a storm and 165 passengers drowned.

We anchored off Bluff, the port of Invercargill, our first call in NZ, and stayed there all day, the ship bouncing and tugging at the anchor. We were waiting for the pilot to take us in when the tide was right. The *Buxstar* was too big to sail into Bluff's small harbour except on a full tide.

Bluff is some distance from the town of Invercargill, separated by an inlet that is crossed by a ferry. It was excruciatingly cold and dreary but I set off to go ashore anyway. A seaman went down the gangplank in front of me to catch me if I fell. There was no wharf bus here so I had to wear a yellow safety waistcoat and walk on a clearly marked yellow line among piled containers and machinery.

This is the south end of the South Island, straight down is Antarctica. It had still been dark at eight in the morning. I struggled in the bitter wind as far as the Seafarer's Centre at the gate but went no further. The weather forecast posted here said that the next day would be a four-layer clothing day. I complied, piling on all I could find on the two days it took to off load and load at Bluff.

When the tugs came to push us out of the harbour, I watched a flock of small birds fishing, diving and swooping into the swirl of water churned up as the tugs grunted against us. The crew had been fishing too and had caught some wonderful big salmon that the cook served up later.

Our next call was Port Chalmers, the port for Dunedin. It was a fine day; the weather wasn't as cold here. There was no wind and the water was mirror smooth. Shore leave until three pm was posted so I galloped off the ship straight after breakfast. At the wharf gate a helpful guard gave me a timetable for the bus to Dunedin.

Port Chalmers is the last stop for those heading down to bases in Antarctica and the nautical museum on the wharf edge had photos and memorabilia from there as well as anything to do with the sea. I saw a large photo of Joseph Conrad and asked if he had been here. But his only connection with this place is that his ship was called the *Port Chalmers*!

I checked out the cosy and well-equipped Seafarer's Centre adjacent to the wharf gate, then sat down to wait for the bus. This day, Saturday, must be the dog's day out in Port Chalmers – lots of owners went by with pooches on leads. Everyone said hello.

The bus driver was amazingly friendly. At first I was the only passenger. He had left the bus when he arrived at the port and wandered away to buy a pie. Then, after we took off, he stopped a little further on and sat in the back seat to eat it. We continued on. He waved to everyone he passed, greeting some of them and most of the passengers who got on by name. He was never in a hurry to take off, waiting until everyone was settled. He seemed to be the local information service as well. No question was fobbed off no matter how long it took to answer.

We rode up and down incredibly scenic picture postcard hills with trees and little wooden houses clinging to their slopes beside fiord-like inlets. But where were the famous NZ sheep? I saw none.

Dunedin was a lot of shops, an impressive church and a street the inhabitants claim to be the world's steepest. I gave that a miss, but strolled about the others.

Later that day I watched the pilot climb up the gangplank as the ship prepared to leave port. It was pulled up after him and we sailed out through the fiords. On high vantage points along the spits of land overlooking the channel I saw cars parked here and there and realised that they had come to watch us leave. On the last headland a line of people stood waving. The crew waved back and I fluttered my hankie, the ship hooted a last farewell and we sailed out into the Southern Ocean.

Soon after that we passed a lighthouse, as lonely as anything could be, on a narrow outcrop of land. From there, there was nothing more until Antarctica. We came to Timaru at about 10 pm, drawing closer to a line of pretty lights, and we were met by a well-lit tug. There was no shore leave here; we were leaving as I got up. But the sunrise was magnificent. At sea it's more impressive due to the open space and the water. This one began with a blood red crimson line along the horizon that lightened and spread upwards until it hit the clouds. Then spectacular rosy streaks streamed all over the pale-blue sky and sea.

Now the weather was warmer and the ship was steady, weighted with the extra cargo we had taken on.

We arrived at Littleton, the port of Christchurch, on Sunday afternoon to be told that no work could start until after midnight Monday. Was this because it was the Queen's birthday long weekend or don't they work on the Sabbath? We anchored in the bay to wait. It was a dreary rainy day, but the calm sea was a lovely pale milky green that became a true aquamarine as the sky darkened later.

Finally we went alongside, passing through many small islands. This bay is the crater of an extinct volcano. Closer in to land there were bare, steep hills that looked mostly uninhabited, and I saw only a couple of houses.

I was so keen to get ashore that I hung over the side watching the gangplank being lowered. But it was atrocious on land. I had to walk a distance to collect the wharf van and the wind nearly blew me into the water. It turned my umbrella inside out and I got wet and cold. Not happy. But the van driver was a cheerful sort who took the other passenger and I through the gate and up to the town without making us stop for a passport check.

The small town rose steeply with all the houses spread out along the hillside. Everyone had a sea view here. The main street sported a few shops and cafes, nothing big. The library was lovely, warm and cosy and full of little kids. I used their internet with a lot of help from a kind librarian. Then it was out into the gale again. In the co-op, a wonderful old health food shop with board floors and brown paper bags, I bought muesli.

I did not try to get to Christchurch; sadly it is a ruin since the earthquake of 2011 devastated it. I found a postcard of the no longer cathedral. What a shame that something so beautiful has been totally destroyed.

In Napier the next day the weather was fairly calm. I went walking towards the town without my umbrella, but the minute I left shelter it began to drizzle rain. The walk along the foreshore of Hawkes Bay, where waves crashed on the pebble beach only a few feet away, would have been nice otherwise. I passed the Seafarers Club and continued on under a row of Norfolk pines that led to the town centre. It was still raining. I came upon a charity shop, nipped in and bought the only umbrella they had – a child-sized one – for a dollar. I ate a slab of lasagne I bought under my small umbrella on a bench in a lovely park where a large Carillion came on suddenly and frightened the wits out of me.

Another couple of rough days and nights followed, the first for a while. One day we passed very close to New Zealand's most active volcano, which sat alone on the sea blowing out plumes of white smoke, bare except for some little green plants along its base. Jutting out of the sea nearby were three skinny pointy rocks, like three guardians.

It was very pretty coming into the Taranga Harbour, our last port of call in New Zealand. Green-covered headlands rose to heights and little boats and buildings hugged the shore. Pushed by muscular little tugs, the work horses of harbours, we were turned around in the small body of water that contained our berth so we would be facing the way out when we left that night.

We crossed the Tasman Sea, then we were out on the smooth Coral Sea, and the weather got warmer, thank goodness. After a short stay in Brisbane, we began passing along the outside of the Great Barrier Reef. Ships travelling this route is not as safe for the reef, but it costs less as a pilot is required for the entire transit of the inside passage. The ship was idling now in order to arrive on time at the rendezvous with the pilot who would take us safely through the Torres Strait.

I was shamed into taking a tour of the engine room by being told that I would hurt the chief engineer's feelings if I refused his kind invitation to do so. I didn't have to like it, though. In fact, I hated it. Climbing down metal steps into the bowels of a ship among mountains of depressing olive green steel stuff did nothing for me. In the past I had seen all the engine rooms I will ever have the need to see. Being told that I was then seven metres underwater didn't help with my claustrophobic memories of the *Poseidon Adventure*. But the two male passengers with me thought it was riveting. Oh well, to each his own. I'll bet they wouldn't get as excited about Tiffany's as I would.

I did, however, absorb the fact that the drive shaft was 90 centimetres wide and that there were ten pistons, whatever that indicates. The chief engineer was a friendly soul and he seemed most proud of his engines, so I assumed a look of interest. He had provided me with gloves and earmuffs for which I was grateful. His engine room was, as such horrible things go, neat and clean, but appallingly hot, noisy and oily.

The agenda for the next day was clocks back one hour and lifeboat drill. I watched the crew launch the lifeboat – not the small man overboard raft but the thirty person fully enclosed boat used for the Abandon Ship lark I kept hearing about. The lifeboat was swung out over the side of the ship with a winch and taken for a run to test its engine. I wanted to get in it for the test drive but was told that swinging out and over and high above the ship is dangerous and is only done with passengers in it in an emergency. Apparently the crew who were used for the test did not warrant such concern! Judging by the time it took to get the boat in the water, we would all have been on the bottom of the ocean by the time it got away from the ship's side. On the third attempt, after swinging alarmingly back and forth on the way down, the boat finally made it onto the sea.

Then it was Emergency Lifeboat drill that the rest of us, crew and passengers alike, had to go through. It was performed on the deck with the lifeboat, having now returned from its little cruise. The alarm sounded and I reported to my allocated muster station as ordered in long pants, sleeved shirt, sturdy shoes, helmet and lifejacket. I spent an hour climbing in and out of the lifeboat in this horrible get-up, and, much to the amusement of the crew, managed to sit in some wet paint.

Next time I will ask if I have the option to go down with the ship. The lifeboat is like Doctor Who's tardis – much bigger inside than it appears outside. I had been sceptical about all of us fitting in there until I tried it and discovered it was indeed big enough, at a squeeze, to take all twenty-two of us. It had all manner of accoutrements like food, water, first aid and instruments I'm sure I could have learned to use if I really had to. But sitting there I had a sudden nasty thought. Where was the toilet? And in particular the ladies toilet! I decided to definitely take the going down with the ship option.

The next day was a lovely quiet day at sea. Towards evening I watched seagulls flying around the mast in front of the ship, swooping and diving as they fished. They looked a long way from shore and I was glad to see them taking turns to sit on the mast rigging for a rest.

Then it was a Birthday Beer Night in the crew mess. Loud karaoke featured heavily in this soiree, compounded by a full drum kit that a junior officer who looked like Ahn Do played rather well. The captain had a good voice and loved to hog the microphone. Everyone sang, even the shy young steward. Lots of beer was handed out. I drank half a bottle of white wine but could not be induced to sing. I actually stayed for three hours, a record for me. I am not a karaoke fan.

After two days of loitering along to keep our date with the pilot, he came aboard from Thursday Island, a long way in a small boat at three in the morning. Then we were transiting the Torres Strait, a narrow passage between Australia's Cape York and Papua New Guinea. On the bridge the captain and five officers were all attention as the pilot called the course. There were islands either side of the channel, which has only a five-metre draught – just enough for the Buxstar at high tide.

Often we were close enough to the Australian shore to receive Telstra and Optus range. Dave, one of the other passengers, stood on the deck outside the bridge talking to his wife in Brisbane.

After eight hours on our ship the pilot was ready to leave, his job done. We were through the Torres Strait. I stood on the bridge watching for the boat that would come out from Thursday Island, one and a half hours away, to take him off. A yellow dot appeared on the bare expanse of flat green sea that soon became the fast-approaching pilot boat. A speedy looking enclosed launch, it was painted in bright yellow and blue. Shaking the pilot's hand, I wished him a safe ride back. He swung easily down the rope ladder that the crew had flung over the side, and the boat sped off into the empty sea.

chapter 11

Once through the Torres Straight it was smooth sailing – bright days and lovely sunsets. I saw a few birds, otherwise there was nothing except the wide dark-blue sea.

The ship's table tennis Olympic finals were held. I attended, but I wished the crew wouldn't treat me like a visiting duchess. When the basketball matches that were held in the swimming pool (dry!) finished, it was filled with water and looked inviting. The large Ukrainian engineer, whom I think I insulted once with a 'Good morning' in Russian, wallowed in it. The pool didn't look much bigger than a large bathtub but a joker had hung a life belt on its side.

The Olympic table tennis finals were won by the divine second officer, Handsome Harry, and the Ahn Do lookalike, and the Olympic Challenge was then held between the finals winners and the two male passengers, Dave and Rick. The passengers won, but I think it was rigged as an act of kindness. I should have backed them when the captain offered me the chance of a bet.

Now the ship was slowly ploughing past many islands, Timor, Maumure, Sumba, Sumbawa, Flores, Komodo, Lombok and Bali, and I started to feel that I had been on it forever. A volcano appeared one day out of the distant gloom of smoke haze that had been colouring everything for a couple of days. The haze was coming from fires that burn every year at this time in Borneo and Sumatra.

Then we began passing other ships that were heading, like

us, to or from, Singapore. One evening we had a barbecue on the deck for the chief engineer who was leaving the ship in Singapore. I got the duchess treatment again and was photographed a lot. More karaoke in the crew's mess followed. This ship was more democratic in the way the crew and officers mixed than other ships I had been on, due no doubt to the gregariousness of our captain.

At last we arrived at Singapore, but only to an anchorage in the harbour where we spent two days waiting for a berth alongside. The ship sat rocking on a calm sea, and, without the breeze of our movement, it became hot and steamy. But there were beautiful sunsets and there was time for another party, this time to celebrate a crew member's birthday and to farewell three others who were signing off in Singapore. Dave, Rick and I were also signing off and were told that immigration would come aboard at midnight when we docked to deal with us. What? Were they mad? Midnight! They did, but thankfully they didn't need to see us, only our passports, which the captain had in his office.

From Singapore I planned to travel overland to Bangkok, where I knew I could get a quick Burmese visa, and then I would fly to Yangon. It had not been possible to obtain a visa before leaving home because the form required proof of arrival and a departure flight. Travelling by freighter makes dates and times movable feasts.

After breakfast we three passengers, farewelled by the crew, left the ship. Our communication with the taxi driver who took us was complicated by each of us wanting to go somewhere different, so he dumped us all in Bugis Street near the city centre. Here I ditched the blokes and as soon as I did, things improved. I found a nice security guard who directed me to the long-distance bus depot. It was close, only four Singapore dollars in a taxi. In fact it was five, but I had only four and the driver gave me a discount. Moral of the story: A woman is better off alone in Asia.

Getting a bus to Kuala Lumpur to connect with a train to Bangkok was easy. The taxi dropped me at the door of the bus company's office and I had to wait only an hour for a bus. Five hours later I was delivered to KL's Sentral train station. Although everyone wanted me to take a plane, I finally convinced the porter who was trundling my bags about on a trolley to show me to the train ticket office.

Only a second-class sleeper was available on the train to Butterworth that night, so I had to take it. This is the only problem with travelling without booking ahead. Malaysian trains run to Hat Yai or Butterworth near the Malaysian/Thai border. Then Thai trains take over, so it is necessary to make two bookings to reach Bangkok.

I had to wait in KL until eleven that night for the train's departure. Checking my bag into the left luggage store, I met a couple of Aussies. I had no money to pay the storeman and the male half of the couple offered me a five Malaysian dollar note, then upped it to ten when I said it wasn't enough. From then on I followed them everywhere. I told them it was because a man who's willing to part with his money so freely should not be lost sight of! But actually it was just coincidence that they kept popping up wherever I was.

They went off to see Chinatown following my directions and surprisingly managed to find it. I met them again later in the station and we were in the same sleeper carriage on the train. We met again in Butterworth station, and on the train to Bangkok they had the sleepers across the aisle from me.

I did not have a very good night. Second-class sleepers are not compartments and their only concession to privacy are curtains across bunks that are tiered in rows down the carriage. Although I was tired after being awake from about 3.30 am when the ship docked, I had an upper bunk and the ceiling light shone in my face, keeping me awake all night.

The train arrived in Butterworth at 8.30 in the morning and I had six hours to wait for the Bangkok train. I tried napping in the waiting room, sitting upright on a hard wooden seat, and woke to find four locals standing in a row in front of me absorbed in the spectacle of my mouth wide open and dribbling. I ate lunch in a workers' cafe outside the station where I was a novelty – 'Kangaroo!' they called to me.

Finally the train came. A young Singaporean man and I shared a seat that converted into bunks later, his on the bottom, mine on top again. The Australian couple I had been stalking ever since he gave me money were across the aisle and a nice hyperactive young American was next door.

We arrived in Bangkok at 2 pm, two hours late. I said farewell to my friends and taxied to the Khao San Palace Hotel that I had chosen because I knew it would be near a travel agency where I could get a visa. It was an okay hotel but they don't trust you not to skip out without paying the bill, so they made me pay up front plus a deposit in case I made off with the towels. Nice sort of people they must be accustomed to dealing with.

The Kao San Palace Hotel may have been okay but the street of Khao San outside it is a nightmare of repulsive tourist activity. I slept for ten hours. And washed!! Two nights on trains and no bathroom. Yuk.

Before falling gratefully on to the bed, I booked a return flight to Yangon with Thai Air International and arranged a Burmese visa application with a lovely girl in a travel agency at the entrance of the hotel. As the weekend was coming up, I had to pay sixty-six dollars for a fast visa. But it was painless and I had it two days later.

I spent four nights in Bangkok. The horrendous traffic makes it slow to get about but taxis are very cheap. And so is food. Drinks were cheap too but not in relation to the food. On Saturday I went to the Weekend Market. It is unbelievably big and crammed with tourist stuff, but also has other goods like fine furniture. It was much bigger than I remembered from the last time I visited, but that was a very long time ago.

I booked the Khao San Palace Hotel for when I came back from Burma, as well as a sleeper on the train south to Hat Yai. Going to the railway station to do this, the booking took a mere five minutes! Getting back took an hour and a half in the bedlam of finding a taxi and getting through the traffic.

My feet were about to do some serious walking, so I tried a fish foot massage. I put my feet into a tank of water containing thousands of tiny fish who nibbled away at them, supposedly removing excess skin. The poor little things had a hard time of it with my tough feet, which were covered in calluses from going barefoot whenever possible all summer, so I had a pedicure to finish the job. The young lady operator took to me with a scrubbing brush and sand paper, more suitable in my case than gentle little fish. I celebrated my new feet with a new pair of shoes. They cost six dollars fifty. And I found a new suitcase that walked with me instead of being dragged. I gave the old one, which was still serviceable, to the nice girl at the travel agency, who I felt sorry for after she told me they work ten hours a day six days a week and get no overtime.

I left for Bangkok airport in a minivan. I was at the airport two hours before flight time as requested by Thai. I complied, having bad memories of what happens when you disobey a Thai Air order. The last time I had flown Thai was in 1988 and though I had vowed, never again, here I was again. They proved to be more agreeable now, but they didn't have the service of former days – no orchids for the ladies, no frills at all. The one-hour flight to Yangon was okay. There were some bumps and cloud but it was soon over.

Immigration at Yangon was a breeze and then there was the young man from Motherland waving a board with my first name on it. An hour's drive to the guesthouse, and what a welcome I received. My room this time was way up on the third floor and not air-conned. It had only a fan, which was fine, it was cool enough. The rate for this room was twenty four dollars, one dollar less than the best rooms which have air-con and maybe even a hook or two.

I heard rain on the tin roof outside my room and, opening the casement windows, I hung out to look at it, revelling in the warmth and fanned by a cool breeze as the rain fell straight down past me. Hearing a tremendous hooting, I realised that I was directly over the train line and there, clanging slowly along to the howling of the local dogs, came the train.

Motherland's ground floor restaurant is long and skinny and its entire eleven-foot frontage consists of wooden doors open onto the street. I sat before them eating my dinner as I watched the warm rain continue to fall softly down in the dusk outside. Now I knew I was back in Burma.

I slept wonderfully, well aware of where I was and very happy to be there. Awake early, I headed for breakfast then walked to the nearby phone shop for a replacement SIM card. They had none and sent me to the Ocean supermarket around the corner where I had no luck either. So I taxied to Chinatown where I was assured I could find one. I still had the phone I had bought last year. After trying several shops, I finally found a young man who inserted a SIM card for me that had on it twenty dollars' worth of calls for twenty-three dollars. Not bad.

I walked about the downtown area thinking I knew where I was but I didn't, so I taxied to the Central Hotel, had lunch in their blissfully cold air-con, then moved on down the road to the Bogeye Market. You get hassled a lot there but it's not unpleasant. I bought a map of Burma, which proved difficult to read as the writing was so small. The Burmese must all have brilliant eyes. Then it was back for a rest – and to watch the rain again.

Dinner in the restaurant that night cost a whole three dollars, but I made the mistake of ordering a fruit salad and got enough to feed a family of eight. Replete, I retired to start reading Charles Frazier's *Thirteen Moons*, which Dave from the ship had given me.

On my last Burmese trip I had travelled around the south. This time I planned to go north. I decided to take it in stages to get to Mandalay – I couldn't face the train arrival time of three am. One of Motherland's ever helpful girls organised a ticket for me on a bus to the city of Pyay, formerly Prome, about halfway. This was achieved with a minimum of fuss and before long I had two tickets for a bus that left at eleven the next day. She even phoned the Lucky Dragon Hotel in Pyay and secured me a room. It has become advisable to book ahead now. Burma has a problem with availability of reasonably priced rooms, so I also booked a room at Motherland for when I returned at the end of my twenty-eight days.

chapter **12**

I left for the bus station at nine next morning in a taxi. It was a very long ride in dense traffic. The two seats I had bought, one for me and one for my legs, were in a big purple bus. The ride to Pyay (pronounced *phewy*), took six hours with time off for good behaviour halfway there. Pyay is situated on the Irrawaddy River north of Yangon on the Bagan Road that follows the eastern bank of the river.

At first we drove through the sprawl of outer Yangon for a long way. Then we followed an almost continual procession of little low village houses and shanty stores and stalls that lined both sides of the road, interspersed now and then with a monastery or gilded stupa. There were trees and grass on the verges and tropic-stained white stone walls.

After about an hour, green patches of paddy began to appear, followed after another hour by large expanses of crops, mainly corn. There were goats and chooks, the odd pig, and many cows. Twice I saw groups of boys sharing a soccer field with a herd of cows. I had been told that cows are so expensive in Burma that they are smuggled across the border from Thailand. They always had a guardian – sometimes a boy would be sitting watching just one cow. If they really are so valuable I suppose it is necessary, but I wondered what it was like to sit and watch a cow all day.

Then it rained; bucketloads of water fell. The pale grey sky along the horizon was slowly obliterated as dense charcoal-black cloud spilled in loops and whorls down into it. This cloud contained more rain that, when we made a comfort stop, descended with a vengeance. The path to the line of loos in the rear of the roadhouse was across an open yard, and a young girl kindly lent me her umbrella.

The roadhouse was merely an open-sided shed containing rows of long wooden tables on which at intervals sat thermoses of tea and hot water and most unsanitary looking communal cups. From the selection of edibles on offer, I bought boiled eggs and a bag of unidentifiable sticks of what looked like biscuit material, passing on anything with claws and legs that could have been insects or spiders.

On the bus music videos played nonstop on a screen that unfortunately, I sat almost in front of. The tapes were long and the songs all sounded the same to me, while the films that accompanied them were mostly of young men and their mothers who seemed to be doing the prodigal son act. After a while this became a bit of a worry. Did all Burmese boys have Oedipus complexes?

I heard spitting sounds and then realised it was people spitting their chewed betel into the black plastic bags that hung by each seat. When full they were left, hanging, for the poor cleaner to remove. Betel chewing was also the cause of much spitting not just on the bus but everywhere, as evidenced by the red stains on footpaths. But somehow this spitting did not bother me like it had in China. It was a different kind of expectorant noise.

At one time the train line ran beside the road and we passed a decrepit train lumbering along with people hanging out of window apertures (there was no glass) or sitting like cattle on open, flat bed trays with metal side rails.

I was pounced on as I climbed down from the bus at Pyay and I agreed to a price for a 'taxi'. This turned into a tuk tuk that bounced and blew me over the poor streets for what seemed much further than the four kilometres I was told it was to the Lucky Dragon.

This hotel turned out to be terrific. It consisted of neat bungalows in a great position on Strand Road, which runs along the riverfront. The view to the water and the green hills on the opposite bank would have been lovely except for the long shed-like building that was being constructed on the other side of the road right in front of the hotel. I asked the receptionist what it was but she did not know. I said, 'It has ruined your view'. She shrugged and said, 'It's the government'. That answered it I guessed.

That night I chomped through a meal of chicken and vegetable, stared at all the way by the entire cast of the dining room and kitchen as I ate with the flat shovel-shaped implement I had been given.

In the morning I was served breakfast that had been fried a long time ago – the eggs were stone cold – and I was presented with imitation orange juice (powdered) but lovely fresh pineapple. The same breakfast almost as Motherland's, but not as good.

I went for an exploratory walk and found a train station in the town close to the hotel. But it was not the one for long distance trains, a pleasant man with a little English told me. He also gave me the unwelcome news that the train to Nay Pyi Taw, where I thought I would go next, left at five am. No way. Buses take twelve hours and leave at night. Even worse! The route is through mountains on not very good roads. I didn't fancy that, so I decided to go to from here to Bagan which was also on my list. The train to Bagan departed at night and arrived mid morning.

I hired a tuk tuk to ride out to the other train station, six kilometres from the town. It was a horrible bumpy grind in an utterly unsprung vehicle and it took a long time. At the station four men lounged on bamboo chaises in various attitudes of repose. These were the station workers. We established that I wanted a sleeper on the night train to Bagan. They assured me that they would try. The train came at 10.30 each night, they said, but it was not always on time. What's new? This did not surprise me. I got back into the wreck of a tuk tuk and we shook, rattled and rolled back to the town again.

Later I walked along the riverside under the shade of trees, some of them huge, up to a bridge about a kilometre or so from the hotel where I had read there was a waterfront restaurant. The river is edged by a low wall, on the other side of which a steep slope runs down to the water. This would be covered later when the river rose with the increase from the monsoon rains. All along here now lay what appeared to be the town's rubbish from the past year, waiting for the water to wash it away. Among the litter, squatters lived in makeshift shelters they had constructed from bits of tin, blue plastic tarpaulins and pieces of bark and bamboo.

It was very hot walking, but the breeze off the water and the trees helped. The traffic along the road beside the river was mostly motorbike and tuk tuk. People sitting on the wall under the trees said '*Mingala ba*' to me as I passed. Halfway to the bridge I saw the riverboat landing. Several large ferries were moored there and out in midstream a barge was being towed upriver. I had hoped to find a boat from here to the north but it was the wrong time of the year. Bigger boats that took passengers only ran north when the water level was higher.

I reached the bridge, a huge long affair on which a car looked the size of a pea. I went into the Southern Star restaurant, which overhung the water. From my seat I could see across to the other side of the river where a small village hugged the shore behind which green hills rose, dotted with a pagoda or two shining golden amongst the greenery. The Southern Star restaurant had a good view of the bridge and river but it seemed to cater mainly to men drinking beer for lunch. No other liquid refreshment could be obtained apart from water. I ordered hot and sour chicken, which almost took my breath away. But the chilli would do me good, I reasoned, so pushed it down.

Returning, I hoped a tuk tuk would accost me, but I ended up walking all the way back to the hotel where I collapsed on the bed and watched Al Jazeera, catching up with the news until it was time for the night market, held in the small street next to the Lucky Dragon. It was a fizz-out as a general night market, but there was lots of food. I bought edible objects on sticks – the only ones I recognised were prawns and they were delicious.

In the morning I fed the little birds outside my room with some of the unidentifiable sticks of food I had bought at the bus stop a few days earlier. I had soaked them for an hour but they were still rock hard, so I stomped them on the ground. The birds sounded and looked like sparrows, but were half the size of the ones I was used to. Two of them were building a nest under the eaves of the bungalow opposite mine. They pulled dry half-metre long strings from the palm fronds of the small trees in the manicured garden between the bungalows.

Then they flew away with the strings streaming out behind them like banners, and ducked in under the building's eaves with their cargo. Large carp and goldfish flashed about in pools that intersected the gardens where a gardener clipped the grass with scissors. I also fed the sparrows the crusts off the awful bread I got at breakfast. The bread was the same I found all over the country – dreadful sweet stuff.

Again I found no transport in the street, so I gave up and walked to Pyay's Shwesandaw Paya in the central area of the town. It was still early enough to be alms gathering (or begging) time and monks and nuns were out in force. A line of nuns, pretty with their pink robes and dark pink wax paper umbrellas, walked barefoot along in front of me. Some were very tiny girls who looked as young as six or seven.

In a commanding position at an intersection in the centre of town is a large golden statue of Aung San, revered former leader, martyred hero and father of Aung San Sui Shi, seated on a horse.

The streets of the town were wide but roughly surfaced. The shops were mostly small and simple, except for the banks, which were grand. I passed the Smile Motel, but it didn't look like it had much to smile about.

I had been walking over the six-foot wide duckboards along the footpaths without realising what they covered. They were gappy and uneven, but until I came to a place where a section was broken and I could see underneath it, I had no idea that flowing along them was a deep stream of sewerage decorated with rubbish. On one side, rows of dilapidated pipes were wired haphazardly to the edges. This was the water supply. It looked worrying. In other places the sewer was covered by concrete slabs that had gaps big enough to fall through.

At the Paya I had to climb up several hundred steps of an enclosed walkway lined on both sides by small stalls selling religious artefacts and souvenirs. This is one of the country's major religious pilgrimage sites. The steps were tiled, smooth and slippery, very narrow and steep. I didn't do so badly getting up although it was awfully hot and airless. My legs had had a good training on the Buxstar's stairs – eighty four up and down at least five times a day. But at the top I discovered that on one side was a large tower that housed a lift. Bugger. I had left my shoes at the base of the steps and it would mean sloshing along in the mud of the street to get back there if I took the lift down. I thought about it, but didn't do it.

The Shwesandaw Paya was possibly built around the 5th or 6th centuries AD and is said to house a tooth and four hairs of the Buddha. An impressive height, the top of its stupa is three feet taller than that of the Swedagon's in Yangon. When I made it to the top of the stairs I walked around the base of the stupa, eyeballed most of the way by a giant seated Buddha statue, the Sehtatgyi Paya (Big Ten Storey) that resides on the hillside opposite.

Coming back down the Pyas steps was scary. I had nothing

to hold onto and I could see the drop below me, along with the possibility of a broken neck. I edged down one at a time, putting both feet on each narrow step. After a while a young woman came and walked behind me, ready to collect me if I fell.

Back on terra firma again much to my relief, I accosted a tuk tuk driver sitting by the roadside. They didn't chase after tourists here. I suppose because we were a rare animal in these parts; I was stared at everywhere I went as an oddity, but not unkindly. I saw no other Western foreigners in Pyay, but I did meet some Thai women tourists in the hotel foyer.

The driver of this glorified motorbike that I had commandeered agreed to take me to see a site that was ten or so kilometres away. We took off, the engine struggling valiantly – it was a lot to ask of a small motorbike engine. But first we went to collect 'my brother', who came too. Was I not to be trusted alone with this young man? The term 'my brother' can cover any degree of relationship up to and including friend. Whatever he was, the two of them looked after me well. They hauled me in and out of the back of the tuk tuk when the going got too hard for me. Mind you, they never touched the nun we picked up, only her baggage. My purity was so far in doubt it didn't matter. They grabbed me one either side and heaved me about like a sack of potatoes.

We rode out on the appalling road of yesterday, past the train station turnoff and into the countryside on dirt roads, crashing and banging. After three hours of this I gave up worrying about my bones and joints. Now my concern was for the damage I was doing to my internal organs.

As we turned off onto the dirt road we were hailed by the little old nun. She wore pink robes and had a large bundle on her head. We backed up and she climbed in over the high tailgate a whole lot more nimbly than I could.

Passing two oxen drawing a wooden cart, we went further

down the road to drop our nun at her monastery, or is it convent, a few decrepit stone buildings without the benefit of doors or windows. I wondered at the privations there. It had an elaborate, garishly decorated entrance gate though. A bit further on was the entrance to the site I had come to see, the ruins of the once enormous ancient Pyu city, Thayekhittaya, which had ruled this area from the 5th to 9th century AD.

Here the government fleeced me of ten dollars hard cash. This fee included an obligatory visit to the museum, which was a total flop – pitch dark and containing a lot of boring old bits of stone.

The route around the city was a dreadful fifteen-kilometre jolting track that took forever in the tuk tuk. There wasn't a lot to see – a city entrance gate, a bit of wall and a couple of red brick pagodas, nothing fancy. Every now and then I was pulled out to go off and look at an item of interest. I liked the pagoda that was a cave, inside which Buddha images hid in secretive alcoves and the big cylinder-shaped pagoda that is said to be the oldest of its kind in Burma.

An ox cart plodded past us on the terrible track. They were making better time than we were. The cart was loaded with great stacks of the leaves that are used to make roofing thatch. My two escorts chewed betel, perhaps I should have too. It is supposed to make tribulations such as this jolting journey easier to bear. I thought they were nice boys until I discovered that one was forty-seven. It should be illegal to look so young. It's downright criminal.

I returned to the Lucky Dragon beaten into submission, a wreck – dirty and with hair everywhere. But still I arranged to go on another jaunt with these two and their tuk tuk the next day. Masochist that I am.

Cleaned up and out on the street again, I found another restaurant overlooking the river close by the hotel on the other side of the road. After recovering from the shock my appearance in their doorway gave them, the management dredged up an English menu. It was very old and in tatters, pages torn in half and all the edges frayed. It offered a couple of odd choices, Fried Sparrow or Fried Insect.

I fancied prawns but got sweet and sour chicken instead. I had not suffered any ill effects from the prawn skewers I had eaten the night before from the street stall, but they had been fried in front of me for long enough to be sterilised. Once again there was no tea or coffee or any other drink but beer. As I ate I watched a small canoe with a square red sail and a large riverboat go by.

After lunch I collapsed on my bed. It was very hot. The rainy season was not well under way yet and this central area of Burma does not get the rainfall of the south that relieves the heat somewhat.

At breakfast the next day, instead of the usual stone cold eggs and hot coffee I was given hot eggs and cold coffee.

Although we had agreed to set off at ten o'clock, my friends were at the gate with their tuk tuk waiting for me at half past nine, so I had to go. The market we had arranged to visit was closed as it was Sunday, but there were still lots of sellers with their wares on the roadsides around the edges of the market. Moving slowly up the narrow street, the driver beeped his horn repeatedly to get a dog out of the way. The dog finally moved slowly just a little to the side, then turned and gave us a most aggrieved look. How dare we!

I told the boys I wanted to buy a pillow for my night on the train. I wasn't sure of a sleeper and a sit-up was likely. So they took me to a shop where they and the entire staff escorted me upstairs. The pillow cost two dollars fifty and was wrapped in plastic. My progress through this shop and up and down the stairs was conducted like a royal tour.

We set off to travel sixteen kilometres south along the Yangon Road to the Shwemyetman Paya – Pagoda of the Golden Spectacles. The green of the countryside was stunning to someone like me from the 'bare brown land'. No dirt at all showed here. The grass grew from the edge of the road, then after a couple of feet it was accompanied by bushes, then later trees, some of them enormous and old. At one place a rice crop was being harvested and several workers in coolie hats were cutting, bagging and loading the hay onto an ox cart beside the road. The road traffic consisted of a great many bikes, motorbikes and the odd cart. Once off the main road the path was dirt but it was not as bad as the one to the train station.

The first pagoda we arrived at had eighty stone Buddha images seated in alcoves in a square, twenty to each side. They were all dressed in gold cloth and had offerings in the bowls before them. An old monk with some English pointed out to me with some pride that they all had their eyes closed except one, but what this signified evaded me. I padded around the site barefoot, now and then on sharp stones that hurt even my tough feet. Behind the shrine there were large aviaries of birds, some were pretty parrots and a couple of the smaller ones looked like budgerigars. And there were several large pens containing dozens of big white and brown rabbits. They don't eat them here so I wondered why they kept rabbits. One resident cat and dog also wandered around.

We moved on to the Spectacles Pagoda. Inside this big pagoda sat a large white-faced Buddha wearing an enormous pair of gold-rimmed specs. And on one side of the gigantic statue was a substantial glass case half full of spectacles. Supposedly put there by cured supplicants, most looked new and unused to me. But, sceptic though I am, I still made an offering here – my eyes aren't what they used to be.

Back at the hotel I rested for the remainder of the day. I had paid for a late checkout at six. I was preparing for my train ride, expecting the worst – that I would have to sit up all night.

chapter **13**

At six I checked out and sat in the hotel's hot foyer on its uncomfortable carved wooden furniture. A little breeze off the river wafted in the open windows and after a while a fan was brought for me. Then, half an hour before I left, it finally occurred to someone to turn on the air-conditioner.

The taxi the receptionist had managed to find arrived. I'd had enough of tuk tuks for the time being. It had rained earlier and the track to the station was difficult even for the taxi. Large pools of water lay like lakes in its ruts and deep holes.

The station was a cement-floored, open-sided stone building covered by a roof, with a small stifling hot office on one side. A few people sat outside on plastic chairs. A station employee wearing only a sarong knotted around his waist came to talk to me. He asked if I was not afraid on my own and offered to come to Bagan with me if I liked. I declined with as much grace as I could. I selected a plastic chair and sat down to wait.

The train was due at ten or thereabouts. At half-past nine the station master appeared. I was surprised to see that he was wearing a smart dark-blue uniform and was smaller than I am. He had walnut-coloured skin, a lovely thick mop of wavy brown hair and the delicately sculptured face of a beautiful ten year old. He summoned me in to the office and laboriously wrote seven copies of my ticket – and gave me the good news that he had been able to get me a sleeper.

I moved to sit out beside the train tracks with the few passengers who had arrived by now. It was a little cooler there. The area outside the office was only a little less stifling than inside it. At a few minutes after eleven, which was pretty good – it's often much more – the train came into sight. The station master hurried up to wheel my bag down the train to the sleeper car. He banged, shouting loudly, several times on the window of the first compartment until the person who could be seen sleeping in there roused and opened the door. It was the train conductor.

The train took off as soon as I had been escorted into my sleeper. It only stops for a few minutes at Pyay. Then, the conductor having been ousted from my bed, I was alone to examine the compartment. And what a surprise it was. I had never seen a sleeper like it before. There were four berths, two upper and two lower, the bottom two as big as proper beds. And hallelujah! There was a private toilet. A door led into the next carriage, but it was locked, so there was no access to the rest of the train. More doors either side of the compartment opened onto the station platform (if we were at a station) or out into the open air! Once inside, the door to the platform was the only way out, but there were levers to pull for help in an emergency.

Before he left the conductor had tried to wrestle the seats down into beds, but not all would comply. I only needed one bed so I chose the one he had been using. It was on the side of the carriage, so that when I lay down my body was alongside an open window. That was the air-conditioning. There was a cupboard with a metal table top between the beds that was beat-up and battered like the rest of the compartment.

Despite the misgivings I'd had about this train and the negative reports I'd heard of it, it was the best train sleeper I have ever had. I lay with the open window level with my face, the breeze cooling me, and watched the stars in the velvet-dark night sky until I fell asleep. Lovely.

At first the train shook and swayed alarmingly and thoughts of derailment occurred to me, especially as the sleeper carriage was the last on the train and we were like the wagging tail of a dog. After a while, though, the movement settled down and the carriage only did the wagging bit now and then. By morning there was just the clicketty-clack of a regular train.

In my isolation I saw no one else on the train until it arrived at Bagan. But I saw lots of people at stations. Even in the small hours of the morning the stations we passed through were alive with people, bustle and noise. I woke now and then to hang out of the window and watch.

Dawn came and the air was still cool. I had needed my cardigan and the blanket provided. Now that we had travelled further north, the country was different. It had changed from green paddy fields wall to wall to sparse greenery with fewer trees and patches of brown dirt – not a sight you see further south. There were small plots of corn, farmers ploughing fallow land with two oxen, and herds of cows and goats and an occasional pig or horse.

The train arrived in Bagan station a little after eleven the next morning, exactly a twelve-hour trip and only three hours late. I took a waiting taxi to New Bagan where I had reserved a room at the Kumundra Hotel. The taxi was a dilapidated, window-less pick-up truck that blew me along in a hot wind. On the way we were stopped at a checkpoint and I had to pay fifteen dollars to the opportunistic government to enter this zone.

The uniqueness of Bagan is that an enormous amount of temples and religious buildings were constructed here. The area is said to have been inhabited for over two thousand years, but the main fervour of temple building began in earnest in 1057 AD and continued for the next two and a half centuries. By 1200 AD there were reported to be over four thousand. Marco Polo wrote about his visit to Bagan in 1298, enthusing over the amount of gold he saw in the temples. The reason for the town's later decline and abandonment is not clear, but invasion by Kublai Khan's Mongol forces did occur in 1274. A great many temples still remain though – a late survey found more than 2200.

At the Kumundra Hotel the accommodation consisted of bungalows lining either side of a central lawn dotted with trees. The extensive grounds were decorated with dozens of randomly placed large glazed jars, with smaller ones resting in tree forks or at their bases. I fell onto the bed in my comfortable room and slept soundly for two hours. My windows looked out toward the swimming pool, but it did not invite me. It was not shaded and outside it was blazing hot, dry and dusty and around 40°C.

I wasn't really enamoured of Bagan. It had an over-touristed atmosphere that I did not care for, and it was difficult to get around. There is not much to do except visit the temples, and they are spread out over a broad plain. Most accommodation is located a distance away, except hotels in Old Bagan which were either grossly overpriced or government owned. Between Nuang U, the transport hub north of Old Bagan, to New Bagan, is a twenty kilometre oval circuit. There are no houses in Old Bagan any longer, only hotels. In 1990 the government forcibly removed the villagers from there to New Bagan, a few kilometres south.

My first visit to Bagan had been very different. It was Pagan then, there was no New Bagan. We stayed in a small hotel in what is now Old Bagan. Being on site, it was easy to visit the temples.

That evening I had a meal on the outdoor tree-shaded area of decking that served as the Kumundra's restaurant. It looked toward Old Bagan where stupas could be seen rising among the greenery of the temple-strewn plain.

I slept some more and in the morning had a good breakfast of fresh fruit salad with a tomato and onion omelette.

Venturing out to the front of the hotel, I was accosted by a horse driver, one of several who wait for custom there on a regular basis. These little carts are the most practical way to get around on the dirt roads and tiny rough tracks, and there are 240 of them in the district.

The driver and I struck a deal for a tour around New Bagan. Just as well I did as it would have proved a long walk along dirt roads in the heat. I climbed in the small wooden cart covered by a hood. Drawn by a small horse, I was clip-clopped up and down the wide dusty streets of the town. It offered little except a few basic stores, a couple of hotels, restaurants and guest houses.

From the town we drove down to and along the riverside, which is nice in a laid-back sort of way. Urged to get out and view the town's gold-painted pagoda, I baulked. They all begin to blur after a while. I was more interested in the horse. A small brown mare with a pink plastic rose on top of her head, she was called Madonna. 'My family like Madonna's music,' her owner, Bo Bo, told me. The horse should be the one to be insulted. Fancy calling a dear little mare after an uncouth old tart like that.

Madonna, Bo Bo and I continued on at a slow jog trot. The little mare seemed tireless. When I got out of the cart I put out my hand for her to smell so that she would know I was harmless, and then I patted her neck. She had stood half the morning outside the hotel waiting for a five dollar fee.

We located the village's travel agent so that I could enquire about a train or boat from here to Mandalay. They knew nothing about trains, but said that boats were not travelling north now except the government one that went once a week. There were no tourist jaunts. I decided that the bus was the best option, especially after I learned that the train left at five in the morning. The bus also would collect me from my hotel. This saved an expensive taxi back to the bus or train station in Nuang U.

Bo Bo took me to a restaurant and announced, 'Lunch'. I did as I was told even though it was only 11.15 am. The people at the eating place were very nice. In an outdoor open-sided pavilion I ordered local red curry. Boy it was hot. I am used to hot and usually it makes my nose run a bit, but this made my eyes water until tears ran down my face. Still, it's good for sterilising the gut – and the nasal passages. For five dollars I got the curry and rice and a plate of peanuts, and some funny looking sweet balls, two bananas and a lime juice were thrown in as well.

Then it was back to my air-con room to recover, passing groups of children walking to school after their lunch break. Girls and boys both wore uniforms of white blouses and dark-green *longiis*.

I rested until evening; it's not advisable to venture out here during the afternoon unless you want heat stroke. Towards sunset I met Madonna and B B again to go temple visiting and watch the sunset from the Shwesandaw Paya, a pyramid-style pagoda whose name means Golden Holy Hair. It has 360 degree views from its five levels and the circular top platform is the most popular place from which to view sunsets.

We jogged a long way on dirt tracks, past brown brick stupas and pagodas sitting among scrubby growth. Then we came to the main road that goes through the village of Myinkaba. Once a large bus passed close to us but Madonna was bomb-proof and didn't flinch. I flinched for her.

The Shwesandaw Paya was a horror of hawkers. They descended on me like a plague of smiling locusts, entreating me to buy as I climbed out of the sanctuary of the cart. I said, 'No thank you' repeatedly, but I did promise to look at one appealing young girl's *longiis* on my way back in order to get rid of her. No such luck. She was waiting at the bottom of the steps when I came down and led me away to her *longiis* arrayed on a wall. I could not escape, so I bought one at the inflated price of seven dollars. Hard bargaining had got it down from twelve. In Yangon it would have been four at the market, and probably two for a local. The girl's cheeks were smeared with the two round patches of thanka that many women adopt. It is powdered sandalwood and is good for your skin, but I didn't understand why it is acceptable to wear it all day. She said she loved my lipstick.

The Shwesandaw is one temple you are allowed to climb in Bagan – not all are anymore, unlike my other visit when we not only almost had the place to ourselves but went wherever we pleased. Then only a few children pestered us, asking for pens.

At the entrance to the site three officials sat at a wooden table to check the ticket I'd bought to enter the zone. Everywhere I went was similarly encumbered with staff. I wondered what they were there to prevent. Whole platoons of boys stood or sat about hotel entrances. Guards or just lookers? And there were never less than three people behind any desk. It took ten to serve breakfast at the Kumundra.

I began the climb. The steps were not for the arthritic or unsteady, but at least there were guard rails alongside them. I used these to haul myself up the steps, which were twice the height of normal steps. The temple is solid stone and rises, cone-shaped, for about two hundred feet in five tiers. On each tier there is a platform and a walkway around the outside. The edges of these have battlements not nearly high enough to appease my acrophobia. It was best not to look down but instead outwards. I made it to the penultimate level, but then my phobia clicked in and I seized up. I stayed there on a corner where the edge was a little higher, still low enough to fall over but at least providing some sense of security if I sat way back from it.

Up there I looked out over the surrounding temples rising from the bushland below for as far as I could see. The view, against a backdrop of a colourful, changing sky, was spectacular.

I sat on the stone floor and after a while a Norwegian tourist who said she worked for a travel magazine joined me. Finally nothing could be seen except the dark outlines of temples against a sky aflame with a glorious red-yellow sunset.

After the sun had gone and the light began to fade, I carefully edged my way down those steep steps, backwards and very slowly, clinging on for dear life to the handrail.

Madonna and I jogged back to the hotel. As we trotted homewards in the dusk I looked back, watching the red sky fade. It was a long way for a little horse at the end of the day. This morning I had asked Bo Bo when we stopped about a drink for her. He had said, 'In the morning and evening.' I should have known that, but I thought in the heat it might have been more.

At the hotel I climbed down from the cart and asked, 'Now home?'

But Bo Bo said, 'Three minutes'. A little rest for his Madonna first.

I had a wash and then dinner. Despite repeating my order of a small fried rice three times, I got a big plate of chip potatoes. When the small rice finally came it was enormous. I'd hate to see the large one. I had a great fruit salad and they made eighty cent fruit shakes that were all fruit, no ice, no sugar. When I paid I added an extra 1000 for the potato chips that I had refused, afraid the little waitress might be fined for making the mistake.

The wifi packed up the next day and the Al Jezira TV station had a signal that said 'scrambled', which made me wonder if something was happening out there in the real world that I was not allowed to know about.

The next day at lunchtime I found Madonna standing under the trees outside the hotel still unemployed, so I hired her to take me to the Green Elephant Restaurant I had read about, situated on the river a little way from New Bagan. We trotted through the town, along dirt roads and down lanes shaded by trees to the river. This restaurant was very posh. At the entrance to it I climbed down and was met, handed a wash towel and escorted inside. The tables were on a deck overlooking the river from where a cooling breeze comes up. The food was expensive by local standards but still only totalled eight thousand kyat. The chicken curry was good and for once it was not huge.

Trotting back, Bo Bo told me that he has one child, a little girl in primary school. He has to pay for this – all schooling costs money in Burma. He also told me that Madonna was ten years old. She had started working at the age of two and her work life expectancy was eighteen. She has had one foal, but work fell off and Bo Bo couldn't afford to keep two horses, so he had to sell it.

chapter **14**

The next night I was talked into visiting more temples. I really would have rather not, but I felt I should support the local economy, i.e. Madonna. I went out at five thirty and there she stood, patiently waiting. We set off and this time Bo Bo took me in another direction to where he said there would be no other tourists. It was dark inside the first temple we came to and empty except for a huge golden Buddha glowing in the gloom. On one side of it stone steps led up an inside spiral staircase to the top of the pagoda.

Bo Bo had pulled out a wooden drawer from under the seat of the cart and extracted a torch for me to see my way up the stairs. Unfortunately it didn't work. He said he used it as the cart's lights when he was on the road at night. Not this night though, I thought. The small emergency torch in my bag also took this time to run out of puff. There was no way I was going up those high, steep and winding steps in the pitch dark, so we moved on down the road, through Myinkaba village to the Mingalazedi Paya.

I was delighted to see that this, the 'Blessing Stupa' was deserted – no hawkers, no tourists. Built in 1284 of reddish brick, it had several terraces that could be reached by steps, but I could only climb up two levels as pad-locked iron gates barred the rest of the way. Still, that was quite high enough for me. I was glad of the excuse to pander to my fear of heights and sit quietly alone for an hour in a cool breeze while the sun declined and an incredible sunset bloomed. The clouds first flushed pink then the surrounding temples and pagodas were back-lit with a marvellous vermilion that then spread over the entire sky. The pagodas darkened until only their black outlines were visible against the flaming red sky. We trotted home in the dusk, sans lights.

Early next morning I was collected by the Mandalay bus. This was a very good deal considering it cost only seven dollars fifty per ticket. For the first time I was travelling with a few other tourists, young backpackers from European countries. It took six hours to reach Mandalay but some of the time was spent collecting or dropping off passengers. The local woman across the aisle was travel sick. She had eaten a big bag of food when she got on the bus. Then she heaved it all up. The woman in front of her did the same.

After two hours there was a halt and some men got off, looking purposeful. When a woman went too, I followed. Behind the roadhouse where we had stopped I stood in the toilet line admiring the establishment's pig, a fine fat sow grubbing happily in the dirt outside her low palm-thatched little sty. I'll bet she did well there on leftovers.

We had a refreshment stop after three hours and I bought a packet of intriguing round yellowish balls. They were terrible, consisting of sugar, possibly flour, and not much else.

In the beginning the country we travelled through looked much the same as that around Bagan. There were goats and cattle and the dirt paths of the villages beside the road were swept clean but any common land was covered with rubbish, mostly plastic. Then there was a stretch of country that was like the area north of Port Augusta in South Australia, with low bushes and scrub and spindly trees. A patch of greener country with large fields of corn or rice followed and after that came some real desert country with reddish dirt and little vegetation.

Finally we were in Mandalay. Founded in 1857 by the

penultimate Burmese king, Mindon, it is not an ancient city. It became the capital in 1861 when King Mindon moved his palace there from Amarapura. In 1885 Mandalay was taken by the British and the last King, Thibaw, was exiled. The fall of Mandalay was said to have been caused by the death of King Thibaw's white elephant. Moral – take good care of your elephant.

I taxied from Mandalay's hot and dusty bus station to the Royal City Hotel that I had booked by phone. I was warmly welcomed with, 'You are very beautiful!' The hotel was five-storeys high and a tiny two rooms wide, with a terrific breezy panoramic roof-top terrace. I loved my corner room with its three wide windows through which the sun shone cheerily. The views included the royal city, so for once the hotel's name was not merely an allusion. Even so, the room had its little faults. An enamel spittoon detracted somewhat from the ambience, and you needed muscular thumbs to turn on the lights. Also, the air-con made a fiendish racket and there was no cold water. This amazed the staff when I told them. It was usually the other way around, with travellers always searching for the elusive hot water. Here I had to speed through the shower before I got scalded.

At the hotel reception desk I had been heartened to find that for the first time in this country I wasn't asked for payment up front. This euphoria didn't last long. It was deflated as soon as I got to my room and read the notice on the back of the door. It said that I would be charged for anything that went missing and a long list of the entire contents of the room followed. And I had thought they trusted me! Was I likely to trundle out with the bar fridge in my bag or a bed or two under my skirt?

I checked out the view of the town from the rooftop. Apart from the royal city walls and the golden dome of a mosque, it was uninspiring, mostly motley-sized worn and weary white concrete block buildings in various stages of decay.

I talked to a German woman up there for a while, and then

I went looking for food. None was available at the hotel apart from breakfast, so I walked to a nearby cafe the reception staff recommended, only to be told that it had now closed for a month. Ramadan had just started so I wondered if the owners were Muslim.

But almost next door to the Royal City I found a Korean restaurant where I got fed – all alone. I ate 'Rice Wrapped', which turned out to be like sushi and was very good. By this time anything would have been. It was a big meal and what I couldn't eat was packaged for me. 'Would you like bar stool?' I thought the waitress said, but it was really 'parcel'.

I had breakfast with the German woman and her family on the roof. They were travelling with a teenager, a boy of sixteen. I don't like their chances, I thought. When the boy left the table they said quietly, 'Never again'.

I walked a long way to a travel agency that I was told changed money. Here I learned the situation with river boating or lack thereof. I had already had no luck with internet enquiries so I gave up on the idea of river travel from here. I tried to find a taxi to return to the hotel but discovered that only motorbikes can pick up passengers in the street; taxis have to operate from hotels. Instead I found a trishaw rider who pedalled me back to the hotel for a dollar.

On the way we passed a Hindu temple, a Chinese temple and a Seventh Day Adventist church. Not far away was St Mary's church, presumably Catholic, and the mosque I could see from my window was close to a pagoda. I was impressed with the seemingly multi-faith acceptance on display in this city.

At four I set off for the night market, following directions from the receptionist. She told me, 'Down the street round to the right'. Well, there was only the wall of the palace there so I walked some more. I got more directions from people in a shop, and I had to cross a four-lane highway with traffic veering all over it. Dodging cars and motorbikes, hoping they would miss me, I made it to the other side. Returning to the hotel, I told the girl I had gotten lost. She looked at me as if I was daft and said, 'Didn't you know to go towards the clock tower?' What clock tower? No one mentioned a clock tower!

I found a trishaw who said he knew where I wanted to go – the night market. He took me a long way to the *day* market. Naturally, this being now night time, it was closed. I walked about the streets but did find some stalls where I bought a wonderful torch for one dollar fifty, the first asking price, but I was not arguing with that. I wished I'd had this torch when I was in the dark temple with the stairs I would have loved to climb.

Another trishaw approached me and I got him to understand that I wanted food. He took me to a Shan restaurant. The food was in open wash-up type bowls arranged along a large table. There were no prices or menu. I pointed to several of the bowls and was dished up a pile of stuff on a plate. An assortment of side dishes and spicy sauces was put on my table and I set to. I ate chicken, snow peas, cucumbers, greens and the tasty but unfamiliar goodies in the side dishes. There was a basin big enough to bathe the baby full of boiled rice to help myself to. It was delicious and all of it plus a litre of water cost two dollars fifty.

The trishaw man had been waiting for me and he pedalled me back to the hotel where we arranged a jaunt around the town for the next day for a fee of ten dollars.

I met him at nine and we set off, me with my umbrella aloft. We passed the police barracks, which was surrounded by a large, old, mouldy white-stone wall on which someone had graffitied in Burmese and English their displeasure with this establishment. There were two English words, one was 'Police', and the other started with an 'F'. Beneath it was a drawing of the Moustache Brother's logo. No wonder the 'Moustache Brothers', a local satire show, have been closed down. I read that going to one of their performances would have got you an all-expenses-paid holiday at a government institution. The brothers have had this experience themselves but continue to perform in clandestinely. Their show casts aspersions at and is a forum for criticism of those in power. It's a wonder they are still alive.

Further on I watched with some distaste a woman using a long-handled plastic dipper to ladle water from the sewer drain through a break in its cover and sluice it around her food hawker's cart to damp down the dust.

The first place I visited was the Royal Palace Fortress in the centre of Mandalay. Built as a one mile square-walled city, this was where the last two Burmese kings had lived. The buildings inside the walls are now replicas; the original ones were destroyed during WWII battles with Japanese invaders. We pedalled along the twenty-six foot high palace wall that is surrounded by a wide moat the size of a river. The wall has four grandly ornate gates, one in each side. Three are forbidden to foreigners, but I was allowed to walk in the fourth after I paid a ten dollar government fee. The palace is now a military compound and outside the gate a huge red sign in English and Burmese said, 'Strike down all who oppose our union', which I found chilling. I would not like to be on the wrong side of this lot.

A heavy presence of uniformed soldiers armed with rifles guarded the tourist gate. Were they expecting an assault by the likes of me? A takeover by a posse of tourists maybe?

Inside the grounds I was confronted by a long driveway. No vehicles are allowed in except the motorbikes for hire that belong there. After a struggle I gave in and let one rider cram a helmet on my head and off we went. There was no traffic so it wasn't too bad.

The palace buildings are stupendous and the grounds are park-like and full of trees. The military compound buildings and King Mindon's tomb are off-limits, but I wandered through a long series of wonderful gold and crimson teakwood halls and pavilions. I saw the 'Glass Palace' where the kings lived and King Thibaw's glass bed. I thought about all the massive teak trees that had been cut down to build this; there were literally hundreds of columns made from tree trunks.

The motorbike rider collected me again, drove me slowly around the grounds, then dropped me back at the gate where my trishaw was waiting.

I did not go to the top of Mandalay Hill, an obligatory tourist experience, even though now there is a lift. I did that last time, the proper way. I think the karma I gained from panting up all those hundreds of steps should still be active. Instead I went to the nearby Shwenandaw Kyaung, a wooden monastery covered in beautifully carved panels. It survived the destruction inflicted on the other buildings of the Royal City because it had been dismantled and moved some time beforehand by King Thibaw after King Mindon died in it.

Next I went to Kyauktawgyi Paya and stood before its massive Buddha, sculpted from one solid block of marble in 1865 – a twenty-six foot, nine hundred tonne goliath for which I bought a string of fragrant jasmine flowers from a small girl peddler.

Then, being my very favourite things, I couldn't miss seeing the world's biggest book. It is at the Kuthodaw Paya and consists of the entire fifteen volumes of the *tripitaka* Buddhist holy text inscribed on 729 marble slabs, each one housed in its own small white stone stupa. The work on this colossal project began in 1857. A paper edition of this text is available – thirty-eight volumes of around four hundred pages each which is estimated would take one person eight hours a day for 450 days to read. The stupas are lined in neat rows in pleasant tree-dotted grounds that lead to a pagoda. There I met a crippled woman who spoke fluent English. She said she had been a teacher but now lived on the kindness of others as she had no family or income. As I am an 'other', I offered some 'kindness'.

At twelve o'clock the trishaw and I were trundling our way back to the centre when I became worried for the rider – it was so hot and he had done much work. I saw a restaurant and called a halt for lunch, mainly to give him a rest. Lunch over, he took me to Mandalay's central Zeige Market (near that pesky clock tower) but, unusually for me, I didn't like it. It was big, crowded, dingy-dark and very dirty underfoot, with rubbish, string and plastic all trying to trip me up. Upstairs was better but boring; the goods were largely all the same.

We pedalled back to the hotel. I was done for the day. Time for a lie down.

chapter 15

At dinnertime I walked down the street a little way, and, sent on my way twice by kind passersby, found the Marie Min vegetarian restaurant. Vegetarianism is something I have studiously avoided since a bad experience with it left me scarred for life. Some years ago I went to the home of a vegetarian man who was trying to impress me by cooking a meal. It consisted of something that was beige and lumpy and smelled like chook food pellets. It tasted worse. It was accompanied by other dishes all similarly revolting, tasteless and foul, one was boiled wheat – did I mention chook food? As if having to eat this awful food wasn't bad enough, it put me in hospital! In the middle of the night I awoke in severe pain from an intestinal obstruction caused by all the gas this fowl food had produced.

Needless to say I never saw that fellow again and the mere mention of vegetarian food still made me shudder. So Marie Min was a revelation. I went there only because the Korean option was closed, but I loved it. Climbing polished teak stairs to a balcony that overhung a tiny lane, I had a divine tomato salad. It was crunchy with onion, nuts and many other tastes and textures, and a big plate of it cost a ridiculous one dollar fifty. It was accompanied by a perfectly acceptable tofu curry and a delicious paw paw lassi.

Across the narrow lane was a Thai restaurant, also on a balcony, so close I could have reached out and almost touched the people sitting there. At this height I was level with the electricity supply of the houses. Wires and connections that looked to be merely extension cords swung in a haphazard tangle in all directions from a central pole. No wonder the electricity was uncertain.

Afterwards I walked back to the hotel alone in the dark street, but I did not feel unsafe. There was still no cold water in my room. The tap that wouldn't turn had been fixed but no water came out of it. The girl from reception grabbed a screw driver, came to my room, applied the screwdriver vigorously, and it was done.

Next morning I set out to find the boat that crossed the river to Mingun, seven miles upstream. Finally I was going to take a ride on the Irrawaddy (now called the Ayeyarwady.) But I vowed afterwards that it would be the last time I went anywhere as tourist infested as Mingun.

My trishaw rider was waiting outside the hotel and he pedalled me to the riverboat landing through the early morning traffic. At the dock I had to produce my passport to buy a ticket – just to cross a river! I was told to wait for at least five more passengers before the boat could leave. It was a fair sized riverboat and we managed to muster up ten takers, all tourists.

The gangplank out to the boat was not for the tangle-footed, consisting of a wobbly plank and a hand rail that was a bamboo pole held between two men standing up to their waists in the water. A helping hand at the other end hauled us on board.

Reclining in an ingenious but roughly made bamboo lounge chair, I watched the wide river flow past, alone in the covered part of the boat where I had a fine view of the toilet whose door had been left open to proudly display the fact that it had a pedestal. The rest of the tourists chose to sit in the sun on the roof.

The level of the river was low and patches of grass showed on the sand bars. On one narrow spit of land in the middle of the river was a rice crop with people and oxen moving about.

Getting off the boat at Mingun was easier than wobbling on had been. We tied up to the base of a temple with white stone steps leading up to the road. Then it was on! We were mobbed by hordes of sellers of postcards, fans, paintings, drinks and dyed quartz pretending to be jade. I dodged around a side path to avoid the mob on the main drag, but was detected by two small girls who pursued me relentlessly until they wore me down. In the end I paid fifty cents for a fan to get rid of them.

The main attraction at Mingun is Mingun Paya, the huge cracked brick base of an unfinished pagoda that would have been five hundred feet tall and the world's biggest if the king building it, Bodawpaya, had not died in 1819 before its completion. Now it is the world's biggest pile of bricks. But crumbling and cracked or not, it was a stupendous sight. In 1838 an earthquake caused a great split in one corner of the stupa and the rubble of bricks that had flowed down from it still sat in a heap at its base. More severe damage occurred last year when a major shock toppled some of the top structure, which also now lies in a mess of rubble at the base. It is said that tourists would have been killed in this fall if the earthquake had not happened early in the morning. The flat top of the stupa used to be a popular spot for viewing the river and surrounding countryside, but now it is forbidden to climb up there. Oh, what a shame, my grateful legs said to me.

I trudged on. Guarding the riverbank are two gigantic stone *chinthe*, half lion, half dragon mythical animal figures. Ten people are said to have lived at times in the cracks in their mouths that were caused by earthquakes.

Following the dusty path that led to the other sites for which Mingun is famous, I walked, dogged all the way by a young boy and girl who said they were in high school. Not today apparently, even though this was a school day. They did not let me escape without relieving me of some of my cash. They had cut me off from the herd the way wolves separate a straggler and wear it down. I try never to buy tourist junk, but I was defeated here and left Mingun with two watercolours of monks and nuns, a swag of postcards, a fan, a bundle of incense sticks and a donation to something – I have no idea what.

I stood inside the Mingun Bell, a gigantic bronze bell cast in 1808 for King Bodawpaya to put in his ill-fated stupa. Instead the bell now hangs from supports in an open-sided pavilion. It weighs ninety tonnes, is sixteen feet across its lip and is the largest intact bronze bell in the world; Moscow has a larger bell but it is cracked.

Two more obligatory payas later and I was gasping for a drink. I had a cup of tea at the stall of a woman who only bothered me a little to buy something, then I went in search of food. At a restaurant overlooking the river I ate a chicken omelette that was a surprise package. It had everything – tomato, onion, eggs, chicken and goodness knows what else, and it cost two dollars.

The boat was supposed to return at one pm but I couldn't find it. The steps we had arrived at were below sight from the shore and I didn't recognise the spot. I tried the main boat landing, but was sent elsewhere. Then I saw two foreigners I deduced must be heading for the boat too, and followed them. I am getting cunning in my old age. Not smart, just cunning. At the landing I met a nice couple, a Chilean man and his American wife. We sat together on the boat and arranged to have dinner later.

Back at Mandalay I saw my trishaw rider waiting for me on the river bank and I gratefully returned with him to the Royal City for a shower and a rest. Boy was I dirty after all the dust and heat of Mingun! I used the 'bottom squirter' to scrub my feet. These hoses on the wall beside toilets are found everywhere in Burma. They are used in lieu of toilet paper. I have never been able to work out quite how, but they do come in handy sometimes.

Later I met Carlos and Beverley, who took me to eat at their hotel. It was in the next street over from the Royal and called The Smart Hotel, which, from what I saw of it, it was. Up on its rooftop bar the happy hour was in progress and I was obliged to drink two free cocktails after which I helped empty several large bottles of beer and dispose of a little food. The view from up there was great. The most impressive building I could see, lit up in technicolour, was the railway station.

My friends insisted on walking me back to my room despite my saying that I felt perfectly safe in this country. Coming out from the air-conditioning of the hotel into the heat of the street was like opening the door of an oven. It had not cooled down from the one hundred plus temperature of the day.

At breakfast I talked to a Danish man who said he was working on something to do with the environment in Thailand. I mentioned the pollution here, but he said that the problem in Burma was not pollution but rubbish. He said that the mentality of the people needed to change but that it would take a long time. In the past it would not have been a problem if the locals threw refuse on the soil because it would have been biodegradable. Now they had to be made aware that you can't do this with plastic.

That day I had made arrangements to hire a taxi driver, a cheerful wizened gnome who lurked outside the hotel on a seemingly permanent basis. I wanted to visit the three former capital cities that are close to Mandalay but too far afield for a trishaw. As it turned out, the driver took me wherever he thought I should go. He was forever smiling and flashing his large gleaming metal front tooth and gold-rimmed glasses at me, and each time he turned his metallic charms on I was dazzled into obeying.

We set off in comfort in his air-conned car and I looked forward to a nice quiet drive in the country. I was soon disabused of that idea. We hadn't gone far before we came to a temple that I was expected to visit. I was put out to walk.

The Mahamuni Paya is a vast complex just south of Mandalay. It has a plethora of entrances, passages, courtyards, pagodas, buildings and shrines – all connected by tiled walkways lined with stalls. It thronged with worshippers, many kneeling before a much-venerated Buddha image – a mammoth, ancient golden statue cast in bronze around the first century AD. The thirteen-foot high statue had been plastered with gold leaves for so long that it was now completely covered in gold to a depth of six inches. Only by men though. No women are allowed to touch it.

In a nearby courtyard one small pagoda housed six bronze Khmer figures that had been brought (stolen) from Angkor Wat. Everywhere I went there were crowds of people. I reflected that you wouldn't find this amount of devotees at nine am on a Monday in any Western cathedral.

Now and then men sat at tables collecting one thousand kyats as a camera fee. I did not use my camera; instead I gave my one thousand to a young man with a withered leg who hobbled about on a crutch.

Then I tried to find my way back to where my shoes and taxi waited. I went down several of the long walkways, streaming sweat in the humid airlessness, but none of them ended in the sight of my shoes. After a while I began to get desperate, thinking that I could be in there all day. I grabbed a man in a dark-green uniform, possibly a soldier, and although he didn't have any English he led me to someone who did, one of the fee collectors. This man took me in tow and trundled me around looking for places I might remember. But it all looked the same to me. He exhibited me to people, and seemed to be asking if they had seen me before. Finally we came to a table of fee collectors who said that they had – how could they forget me, the weird foreigner? – and pointed in the direction I had come from. Just then, my driver appeared. He had been searching for me, realising I had been missing for too long. I shook my guide's hand fervently in gratitude for my deliverance. I really wanted to kiss him, but I controlled myself. He was probably saying, 'Silly senile old bat'.

Back on our tour the cheerful gnome asked if I wanted to see the monkeys fed. I said yes, I loved monkeys. But this was another misinterpretation. It was not monkeys I was taken to see being fed, but monks.

At a gigantic monastery for novices, thousands of monks had their one meal of the day at this time. Poor things. I imagined how I would feel with only one meal a day. Having tourists gawk at me as I ate this meal would have made me feel even worse. Busloads of tourists are brought here to witness this treat.

Along the shaded pathway of the monastery, two very long rows of monks were lined up waiting to go into the refectory. The tourists stormed in, cameras ready to photograph them while they ate. How disgusting. I would have none of this. I left. Would they like a busload of Japanese tourists descending on their homes at tucker time and photographing them like animals in the zoo?

We visited more temples and monasteries, where I was pushed out of the cool sanctuary of the taxi to trudge about in the heat barefoot. Where was this drive in the countryside I had set out on?

We arrived at Sagaing, an ancient capital of a Shan kingdom that had arisen around 1315 after the fall of Bagan. It is now a major religious site with five hundred stupas and six thousand monks and nuns. We drove, thankfully, up Sagaing Hill on a high, winding, narrow road lined both sides with low white stone walls. Where the road ended the steps began. I climbed up many, many steps to look down on to a wide vista of green hills, their slopes dotted with a multitude of gold or white pagodas and stupas. I climbed slowly, stopping often at the seats provided to absorb the restful atmosphere the close growing gardens and overhanging trees afforded. Not to mention to absorb more oxygen into my complaining lungs.

Near the top of the hill, forty-five colourful Buddhas sat in a peaceful crescent-shaped colonnade looking down to the distant river. Further up was the ninety-seven foot high Soon Uponya Shin Paya that was built in 1312. I liked its donation receptacles – waist-high bronze frogs that I couldn't resist stroking.

At Amarapura, City of Immortality, the royal city before Mandalay, not much could be seen of its former prominence. Most of the palace buildings had been dismantled and moved to Mandalay when it replaced Amarapura as capital. The main attraction here now is the wonderfully picturesque U Bein's bridge. The longest teak bridge in the world, constructed of sixteen hundred sturdy teak posts, for two hundred years it has provided a way across the wide, shallow Lake Taungthaman to the village on the other side.

I needed restoration again so I sat in a bamboo chair at a nearby outdoor tea house to admire the bridge, which stood high above the water of the lake with villagers and monks walking along it. As soon as I stopped I attracted a hawker, a young girl who softly and gently harassed me to buy her pseudo jade jewellery. Suddenly she leaned in, stared and pointed to my hand. I wasn't going to try to tell her about it, but then she showed me her hand. She had a long scar very similar and on exactly the same place. (No one in Australia ever asks me about my scar. Don't they see it, perhaps they just don't care.) Examining her little hand, I saw that it was useless, all twisted into a claw. She said, 'Operation'. She had few English words but this one she knew only too well. Then she showed me her leg. It was also deformed and scarred. I could not diagnose what had caused this, but I know that anyone disabled in this country is unlucky. I bought her jade lookalike at an exorbitant price.

chapter 16

Now it was time for lunch and my guardian took me to a simple restaurant, open on all sides but roofed and well supplied with plastic chairs. The bamboo shoots and chicken I ate was very good and cost two dollars with a fruit juice. I could never get over my surprise at the cost of food in Burma. Hotels and guesthouses might be going up in cost by the hour, but food remains the bargain of the century.

Continuing on, the taxi left me at a riverside landing so I could take the ferry across to the other side to visit Inwa. The driver said he would wait there for my return. Inwa, formerly known as Ava, had been a Burmese capital city for four hundred years.

The ferry was a small wooden boat with an outboard. That is the other great bargain in Burma – transport. The return journey cost eighty cents. On the opposite landing I had to hire a horse cart to go around the sites. I shared one with Emily, a pleasant young American I had just met, and we bounced and shook over little dirt tracks for the two hours that this expedition took.

We visited a couple of stupas and then a large teak temple, accompanied all the way by would-be sellers of trinkets who smiled and laughed and said, 'Later' when we said, 'No thank you'. Perhaps they were familiar with the wearing down capacity of sheer persistence. This time, however, I was strong and managed to resist.

Bagaya Kyaung, the teak monastery, was constructed

entirely of teak wood. Wonderful carved panels and huge columns up to sixty feet high decorate its interior, which is dim and dark except for a golden idol shining in its innermost recesses.

Waiting for the return boat, Emily and I sat at a table under big flame trees by the landing and drank fresh mango juice. Emily, although of a different generation from the older American couple I had met in Mandalay, without any prompting said exactly the same about the folks at home – that most were uninterested or ignorant about the rest of the world or travelling, especially to Asia.

Back in my taxi, the driver took me to an Ocean Supermarket to restock on cheese before releasing me to rest. At six I resurfaced to walk to Marie Min for another tomato salad and lassi. It was still very hot. Marie Min confirmed that SIM cards for phones had been super expensive just a year ago. I had found it hard to believe that they could have been one thousand US dollars, but she said it was true. I suppose it had been the government's way of restricting access.

I would have loved to take the scenic railway to Pyin U Lwin, formerly Maymyo, where I intended to move to next, but it left at the ridiculous hour of three in the morning, so I opted for a share taxi instead. It collected me the next morning and I was put in the front seat. We weren't far into the journey before I was fumbling frantically for the seat belt. Surprisingly it was functional; mostly they aren't. In the back seat were two Burmese ladies and a child. All we could do was smile at each other after I had exhausted my Burmese conversational skills with '*Mingala ba*'.

After travelling through the town, heavy with pollution, bikes, motorbikes and cars, we were soon on small roads overhung with trees so it felt as though we were going through green tunnels. Now and then, lines of dirt-coloured shacks or a row of bamboo, woven rattan and thatch stalls edged the road. We stopped for petrol and were each given a bottle of free water, a general practice at service stations in Burma. But what about all the waste bottles that were thrown into rivers and onto the land? Beside the petrol pumps stood a utility with a double-decker load of bamboo crates holding a cargo of pigs. I was pleased to see the driver giving them a long hosing down. Pigs don't handle being overheated well.

Then the road began to climb into the mountains. It was a relief to see that the old, narrow winding road I remembered from before had been supplemented by another road travelling in the opposite direction, making it two-way. There were not many villages on our path and only one town, which was good as our driver did not slow down in the least for any of them.

We reached Pyin U Lwin in one and a half hours. I had booked a room at the Royal Park Hotel, out of the town a little in the gardens area. Here I received the usual enthusiastic welcome. My room was not ready so I sat on their comfortable veranda to wait. Surrounded by flower gardens with orchids hanging from large trees, birds chirruping and frogs croaking, it was blissfully cool and green.

Maymyo, now Pyin U Lwin, was a British hill station established on the site of a small village in 1896 as a place for the colonial government administration to escape the heat of the plains. After the railway from Mandalay was completed it became the British summer capital until the end of British rule in 1948. It is a delightful little town, famous for its colonial houses, great fruit and vegetables, jams and juices and the National Kandawgyi Gardens. Established in 1915, the gardens cover 176 hectares and have 480 species of plants.

That evening I dined in solitary splendour in the hotel restaurant. Seeing rum sour on the drinks menu at one dollar fifty, I asked to try it. This caused an excited twenty minutes of flurried to-ing and fro-ing between the kitchen and the desk before it arrived, in a very fancy cocktail glass, although without the standard paper umbrella that came with ordinary fruit juice.

That night I had a wonderful sleep. It was so very quiet here. During the night it rained heavily and in the morning I went walking to the town in the cool, fresh air. It was a fair distance but the road sloped gently downhill and was shaded by a canopy of big trees. Undergrowth and greenery lined the edge of the road I ambled along, admiring the trees and flowers. Then a motorbike went past and the rider yelled a word *twice* and pointed to the road in front of me. There, slithering sinuously with evil intent across the road directly before my feet, was a snake about seven feet long. It was thin and shiny-black, so I know it was not a python. It was probably one of Burma's numerous deadly lot that I had read about. I waited for it to disappear into the undergrowth and from then on paid serious attention to where I was putting my bare, sandal-clad toes. Tomorrow I will wear boots, I vowed.

When I reached the town it seemed much bigger than I remembered. It even had a stop light now. I walked along the main street, the centre of which is dominated by a clock tower that was a present from Queen Victoria. I found a bank with a decent exchange rate for the US dollar. I was served by two charming boys and checked out the price of gold in the goldsmith workshops. I visited the market that sprawls over a large area close to the main street where stalls were piled high with local specialties – fruit, jams and organic coffee from the Shan hills. Several old people asked me for money, some of whom seemed to be Shan. I bought a small light. The Royal Park Hotel was great but the lights were up, fourteen feet away, in the ceiling.

At the Tourist Information Office, I found a woman who was most obliging, contrary to reports that say these places are most often useless. She took me next door to a bus office and helped me buy a ticket on something that previously I had been told by several people didn't exist – a daytime bus to Nay Pyi Taw. I wanted to go there next but had been offered the options only of a night bus or of going back to Mandalay and starting from there. The moral of this is – you need to ask many people to find the correct answer.

Nay Pyi Taw, which means royal capital, is Myanmar's new capital city that the government in its wisdom (or otherwise) decided to create in 2005, supposedly on the advice of their official fortune teller.

I rode back to the hotel in a buggy straight out of Cobb and Co, an old wooden mini stage coach. These are the usual method of transport in Pyin U Lwin unless you want to ride pillion on a motorbike.

At dusk I sat on the hotel balcony. The mosquitoes were very bad then and a waiter lit a repellent coil under my feet, which, combined with catnip drops behind the ears, helped to fend them off. Horse carts arrived at the hotel, delivering tourists back from day trips. The horses generally looked in good condition and well cared for, but I watched one poor little animal panting, recovering from the effort of drawing two great lumps of German womanhood up the hill slope.

The local fruit here is made into terrific juices so I ordered papaya juice with a shot of the ubiquitous Mandalay rum as a variation on the rum sour, and received a giggling response from the waiter.

Next day I walked to Candacraig, where I had stayed on my first visit to Burma. Now closed, it had been privately run and was then taken over by the government who reputedly made a hash of managing it. It was now about to be resurrected by a local company. It was not far, and I made my way there along undulating forest-shaded roads. Every now and then I passed a big old European-style house that appeared quite out of place in Burma.

The exterior of Candacraig looked old and sad. Pine needles lay thick on the shingled roof and head-high weeds flourished where the once-lovely gardens had been. But flowers still struggled to push their blooms up among the weeds and inside the marvellous polished wooden floors still gleamed. A caretaker, on her knees busily shining them, smiled up at me. I walked slowly around the carriage drive, which years ago pony carts had trotted smoothly along; now it was rough and pitted with potholes.

Down the road a little I found a horse cart to take me to the town. Riding in one of these relics was rather like being in a rustic, rattly old hearse – from the corpse's point of view – in the coffin. You can't see out unless you lie down. The cart was covered overhead and all around except for glass-less windows low on the sides. And, surprisingly, instead of an aperture through which to see the driver ahead, there was a mirror. So you sat there with your travel-worn, frazzled face staring back at you. Not a morale booster.

In the town I met a girl I had spoken to in passing the day before – a poet from Luxembourg. I stopped and had some local coffee with her while she read me the poem that she had just written in the botanical gardens.

Another horse cart took me back to the hotel, this time by a different route that I think was not so steep for the horse. On the way we passed a Hindu temple, a large Christian church, a pagoda and a Chinese Buddhist temple. A mosque occupies a dominant position in the main street. Pyin U Lwin's Hindu and Muslim populations are descendants of the Indian workers brought here to work on the construction of the town and the railway.

That night the rum got lost in translation and I ended up with straight papaya juice. Or was it that they were trying to keep me wholesome?

The bus to Nay Pyi Taw left at 10.30 in the morning and I was the only foreigner on it. At first it was cold as we came down through the mountains, which were green but not forested. I wondered if all the trees were in the temples I had seen. The mountainsides were covered in low scrub, creepers and bushes.

I saw that horses were still used as transport in the villages and towns we passed through down as far as Mandalay.

We didn't go into Mandalay but veered off on a side road. The bus stopped after a couple of hours and I bought a packet of chips and ate the banana sandwich I had made in the hotel from the breakfast provisions. After we came down onto the plain and the sun was on my window it began to get warmer.

I didn't know that this bus did not terminate at Nay Pyi Taw and goodness knows where I would have ended up if I had not suspected that we had arrived. Hanging out of the window, I asked, 'Nay Pyi taw?' It was. I took a proffered taxi whose driver quoted me a price that I thought excessive until I saw how far we had to travel to the hotel I had phoned ahead for a room. I was stunned by the distance between places in the town. Even though I had read about this, the reality was a shock. And what ran continually through my mind as we drove endlessly through empty spaces was – why? What reason could there have been to build a city like this? They could have taken notice of Colonel William Light's great plan of the city of Adelaide, still lovely and functional after one hundred and seventy seven years. Built on a square mile grid with a mile of public parkland all around it, it is a very sensible city.

The taxi took me a long way, several miles at least, along a six-lane highway absolutely devoid of traffic. On both sides was green, empty bush edged with newly planted trees and centred by a median strip filled with flowering bushes and shrubs. When the trees are avenues they will be lovely. But why all the open country of bush between everything? After twenty minutes of fast driving I saw the first building, a massive hotel, then there were more half-finished three or more storeyed buildings. More open space followed, as all the while we travelled along these great wide highways, intersected now and then by big, high roundabouts topped by a gigantic rose, in one place red, another yellow.

Finally we came to the hotel zone, one of the several separate zones into which the city is divided. All foreigners have to stay in the hotel zone and some zones, like the one for government buildings and the generals' houses, are off limits. There are some colossal hotels in the hotel zone, each surrounded by large grounds, trees and neon lights. The Tungapura, the almost-new hotel I had booked, was great. Superficially. Flaws appeared on closer inspection. The marble wash basin was cracked, some lights didn't work, and the elaborate fancy curtains wouldn't draw without considerable assistance.

For the first time in Burma the hotel asked to be paid in kyats, telling me that if I paid in dollars it would be converted at an abysmal rate. I had just enough kyats for one night, but the next day was Saturday and the bank was closed. 'Oh, well,' as Scarlett O'Hara said on the last line of *Gone with the Wind*, 'tomorrow is another day'.

My room on the first floor had terrific lights, even with some not working, and wide French windows that opened onto a ledge that looked as though it had been designed as a small balcony. But its edge was only four inches high. No cattle prod on earth would have got me out there. The hotel foyer was marvellous and there were real plants here and there; even in my bathroom there was a pot of devil's ivy. The bathroom was big and had a washing line that could be pulled across it. Now that really is encouraging washing. I complied and soaped up a storm.

Later, as the sole diner in an empty expanse of restaurant, I provided entertainment for the two lonely waitresses. Then I slept well despite being lost in a king-sized bed.

The next morning, after a substantial buffet breakfast, I asked at reception about transport. There was no public transport or trishaws, only taxis at fifteen dollars an hour. This was dear by Burmese standards but there was no option here. I had to use a taxi. The driver spent an hour trying to find a money changer for me. First he took me to the supermarket, a huge shopping centre in the shopping zone and a fifteen minute drive from the hotel section, again through open country on massive freeways. At the money changer there the staff didn't have the key to the money box! I waited, but when the person who should have had the key was located, she couldn't find it.

The taxi driver took me elsewhere. This involved another long drive to where the town zone is located, a further ten minutes away on a freeway also lined with trees and with open green bush-covered land in between. The town wasn't much, only a few shops, some empty, a collection of new-looking houses and a small market. The money changer was located in a private house and we did the deal in the street, which reminded me of the old days of my black market career in Burma.

There were not many attractions on my Need to Visit list for Nay Pyi Taw. I had come here mainly to see what a new town built on the recommendation of a sooth-sayer looked like. I had heard it was weird. It was.

So I went to the museum, the waterfall park and the stupa – at all of which the government did its utmost to extract as much money as possible from me. At the waterfall park I had to pay a fee just to get in the gate. It covers a large area and has many trees but it was really nothing special. The stupa looked the same as they all do except this one was new and much decorated. It was also extremely high, but this time, fortunately, I found the lift. Before I was allowed to go up in it I had to pay two thousand kyats for the use of a *longii* over the trousers that I was wearing. I had forgotten I would be visiting a holy place. This *longii*, which they thought I might not be able to resist taking home with me if I was not charged a deposit fee, was a dreadful old rag. I should have charged them to put it on me!

And my handbag was searched! This is not a job for the unwary. I wondered what they thought I was hiding in there. Did they expect terrorists in a quiet paya in this isolated part of Burma?

Up on the forecourt of the stupa, many people walked, circling it, but it was very windy so I hastened inside. The interior was magnificent, with large expanses of glittering floor tiles and shining gold statues abounded.

Continuing on in the taxi, another long drive brought me to the City Hall. More a series of extended palaces, I could only admire it from a distance as it is forbidden to foreigners, as are many other areas of the city. I wasn't even supposed to photograph it, but I did.

Nay Pyi Taw was not an easy place to visit as a tourist. Unless you brought your own transport or were prepared to pay large amounts for taxis, it was impossible to get about. The only other visitors I saw were Chinese or Indian groups on business tours.

I paid off the taxi at the supermarket and spent an hour and a half in there. I bought a bus ticket to Inle Lake, in central Shan province, my next port of call, and obtained some more money from the girl at the money changers who by now had organised the cash box. I had realised quickly that I needed more money in this expensive place.

I ate cold pizza and drank a watery milkshake sitting at a table in the supermarket cafe, accompanied by a young man who practised his English on me. He worked at one of the hotels. I assumed that all the people in the city would have been brought here to work. I saw no people on the streets like in other towns.

The ticket I had bought was for a night bus. I had sworn I would never take one of these horrors, but there was no other way to get from here to Inle Lake. In anticipation of this event, I bought another pillow in the supermarket. I had given the one I had bought for the train to the receptionist of the Royal City in Mandalay.

Then I returned to my very comfortable hotel room and

settled in, vowing not to move until it was bus time. It was simply too hard to get around and there was nothing much to see except those immense freeways and wide empty spaces.

After checking out of the hotel at twelve the next day – and paying for the glass I broke! – I sat in the foyer until five when it was time to go to the bus station. The staff put on the TV for me and a young and very beautiful male receptionist came to talk to me. He said his family were in Yangon and that all the staff lived in the hostel. I had noticed this less than posh building at the back of the hotel, separated from the paying guests by a big fence covered with green shade cloth. Where else could they live? The hotel zone was utterly isolated.

I had expected a grand new bus station, but the government apparently is not interested in bus travellers. They want cashed-up flyers. There was nowhere under shade to sit except up some steps in a daggy little office. My bag was left down in the street beside a stall selling packets of munchies. You wouldn't do this in Thailand or many other countries. When the bus arrived it was not as good as the last two I had taken. The seats were tiny and rock hard and they did not recline. If I stretched out my legs I had only half my bottom on it. Thank goodness for my pillow. Though each seat was provided with a green-frilled baby pillow, they weren't much use except to help insulate you from the sharp arm rests. We left the bus station on the dot of six, but it was half past seven before we got away from Nay Pyi Taw.

chapter 17

There were three bus stations, all miles apart, in Nay Pyi Taw. We called at them all collecting passengers, as well as a village on the outskirts of the city where there was a market and some normal-looking Burmese houses.

Outside my bus window an almost full moon was rising and I fell asleep watching it. Despite my fears of spending a sleepless night on a bus, I was snoring long before half-past eight. I woke up then because the bus had stopped for our first feeding and toileting session – a whole hour had elapsed since our last pick-up stop. This is going to be a long trip, I thought.

Everyone had to get off and we were locked out of the bus until the driver returned. The next stop was at eleven-thirty and the same procedure followed – more food, more toilets. Then the old bus began labouring up steep winding roads into the mountains. Halfway to the top we pulled off the road at a place where several buses and trucks stood in mud and puddles while their drivers hosed down their tyres, cooling them in preparation for the rest of the ordeal.

Continuing on with cool tyres, grinding and bumping in an ever-winding ascent, we arrived at the top. I slept again and woke when we had our last stop for refreshments at half-past one. An hour later we seemed to have arrived somewhere. People had been getting off along the way by calling out to the driver to stop, but this place looked like a major halt. Wherever it was, everyone got off, so I did too.

I showed someone the ticket that had on it my destination,

Nyaungshwe, the closest town to Inle Lake, and received the unwelcome news that I had come too far. The bus driver had not realised that I had no idea where I was and that the road signs I had seen, being in Burmese script, had told me nothing. The driver's assistant, who had been told by the ticket seller in Nay Pyi Taw to put me off at the Nyaungshwe turn off, had disappeared somewhere along the way. A man who spoke English was found to talk to me. He said I could take a taxi back to Nyaungshwe, and a vehicle was promptly found. It was a long way back. The taxi, a decrepit old heap on its last legs, bucked, jolted, creaked and groaned over the bumpy road, innocent of windows, which was handy for the spitting. Not me, the driver, who was chewing betel and seemed to be having trouble with his eyes. He slowed to a crawl when cars or trucks with lights approached.

Now and then we passed people walking along the roadsides, even though it was almost four o'clock in the morning. I had noticed that people were always out and about at all hours of the night. I suppose this explains the ludicrous train and bus times.

From the turn off on the main road, another long road led to Nyaungshwe. Arriving there and asking directions, the driver got me to Teakwood Guesthouse where I had booked a room. Despite the hour, a woman soon opened the gate. In the semi-open office area two young people lay sleeping on old grey blankets on the cold tiled floor. 'My staff', she said to my enquiring look. Poor kids. Apparently a tough employer, she was a brittle woman, not at all like other Burmese women I had met who were soft and gentle and kind. I did not take to her. However, right then all I wanted was a bed. Desperately.

From a monastery across the road a very loud chanting bellowed out nonstop. I asked for a room at the back further away from the racket and was told that this would cost more. Upstairs was even dearer. And yet, value wise by Burmese standards, this was a twenty dollar hotel! They didn't even supply a bottle of water or a glass if you had brought your own. Thank goodness I had the bottle the bus company had given me; a miss-spent youth drinking beer from bottles serves me well in times like this.

I slept until after eleven and got up, bleary eyed, for lunch. It was hard to believe the difference between the wonderful Tungapuri hotel I had just left, that had cost only two dollars more, and this place. The 'nice garden' of the Teakwood's blurb was for me a fine outlook onto a couple of clothes-drying racks laden with crumpled washing. And as for that chanting! The same phrase shouted with the aid of an amplifier over and over very loudly. It did not stop all day as this was now a special time of Buddhist lent. I am not adverse to a bit of chanting, but I began to fantasise about marching over there with a big pair of scissors and cutting the cord of that amplifier, or at least pulling the plug.

Unfortunately I had been pressured into paying up front for three days when I arrived, otherwise I would have moved.

Towards evening I ventured out. I was told that it was only a five minute walk to the main street of this small town and surprisingly it turned out to be true. It isn't always. The street contained small cafes, shops and boat tour offices. I arranged a boat trip on Inle Lake, an obligatory exercise when visiting this area, with a friendly man whose smile displayed betel-destroyed teeth and blood-red gums. Nearby was a bank with a money change office, but it was not open until morning. Outside it stood a brand-new ATM, the first I had seen in Burma.

Nyaungshwe is situated at the end of Inle Lake, connected to it by a canal, and is the commercial hub for the villages dotted around the lake's edge. I ate at an outdoor cafe but moved as soon as I could to escape the increasingly persistent and ardent attention of the local mosquitoes. In the street I stopped to talk to a Belgian family with two small blond children. Their mother said that the children were fussed over wherever they went and everyone wanted to touch the smallest one, a little boy, which naturally he hated. In a tiny bar I bought water to make up for the Teakwood's inadequacy. It would not have cost them much to provide it; a one litre bottle was less than thirty cents.

Despite the chanting, which continued all night, I slept. Ear plugs and exhaustion helped. In the morning I changed money at the sparkling bank, the only posh building in the town. It took three uniformed guards and three tellers to do so. The rate I received was the best yet, 983 kyats to the US dollar.

I presented myself for the boat trip and was introduced to a young man, Kyaw, whom I was told wanted to be my guide. I didn't want a guide. They mostly mean well but have so little English or such a peculiar accent that they are usually incomprehensible and serve no useful purpose. I was told, 'You don't have to pay him, just tip him if you like him'. Terrific. I was in no win situation. But everyone in this country needs employment, so I agreed that he could come with me. I had no idea what a tip should be but I had learned that, unbelievably, the average daily wage is one thousand kyats.

We set off – walking. I was not amused. It was already hot and it was a long way to the canal. 'I thought there was a boat involved in this deal,' I bleated, trotting to keep up with him. But then, there it sat on the canal, a long, skinny, blue-painted wooden canoe. It had no covering but there were two chairs low down in its bottom where Kyaw and I sat in single file. The driver perched up in the rear with his outboard engine, I popped up my umbrella, and we were off.

It took half an hour to zoom down the long canal that connects Nyaungshwe to Inle Lake. The first part of the canal is lined with houses, guesthouses and shops, all wooden. Then we were on the lake where the breeze was delightfully cool. Mountains ring the lake all around, green and devoid of anything but their folds. Villages cling to the shores, their wooded, bamboo and woven rattan houses on stilts high out of the water; the level of the lake was low at this time as the wet season increase had not yet arrived.

Inle is a shallow lake with a surface area of just under fifty square miles, the second biggest in Burma. It took another half hour to cross to the Phaung Daw Oo Paya, the holiest religious site in the south of the Shan state. The boat pulled up to a landing from where reaching the pagoda involved a long trek on wobbly wooden walkways elevated over water and mud. There were loose boards underfoot and wonky bits of loosely applied bamboo for hand rails. I proceeded with caution.

At the pagoda a huge crowd wandered about. The full moon festival was in progress. This Paya's holy treasures are five small ancient Buddha statues that have been plastered with gold leaf over such a long time that now they are unrecognisable blobs. Kyaw told me that one has increased in weight by several kilos.

This day was a time to offer flowers. Kyaw encouraged me to buy some lotus blooms and then he made an offering of them in front of the appropriate statue. Kneeling, he bowed his head to the floor three times with my flowers clasped in his hands. A woman approached Kyaw with two pieces of gold leaf and asked him to apply it for her. Only men can step up onto the dais on which the statues sit to make offerings or put gold leaf on them. A sign beside it said, 'No ladies allowed'. My mother was finally vindicated. She was always telling me there were things ladies could not do but I never believed her. Mind, you wouldn't find me buying gold for an idol that thinks it's too good for me to touch it. Get your own gold, I'd say.

Moored beside the pagoda in a covered dock was a big, glittering golden boat with a prow in the shape of a *hamsa* bird's head. Once a year it is used to ferry the gold Buddas around to all twenty-five lakeside villages to spend a night in each. Originally all five statues went walkabout annually, but in 1965 the boat capsized in a storm and all the Buddhas went to the bottom of the lake. Four were recovered and one was left to be searched for again in the morning. But on returning the four to the pagoda, the fifth was found to be already there, waiting for them. The next year the same thing happened – a storm and a lost Buddha returning of its own accord. Then the people got the message that the fifth Buddha did not like to travel and so now only four go on their little annual holiday of twenty-five one night stands.

I was surprised when Kyaw told me that he firmly believed this. There *was* a storm because there are photos to prove it, but as to the rest … Oh well, lots of people believe far more unlikely Christian miracles. But I did like the way Kyaw bowed and prayed at each site we visited. An unbeliever can still take pleasure in someone else's trusting faith.

Outside in the grounds we joined a throng of people pushing their way through a packed market. There were Shan and other ethnic people in colourful traditional dress patronising the tea houses and eating places that offered their particular food, along with stalls piled with many kinds of fruit, spices and local produce.

Back in the boat, we moved on to the fisherman's village, with me resisting all offers of visits to weavers, silver smiths and any other place where I knew I would be pressured to buy stuff I didn't want. Like ship's engines, I have seen enough workshops to satisfy me for the rest of my life. And especially I did not want to see the Paduang, the 'long necked women', who have had iron rings placed around their necks until they are deformed. They are on exhibition at one of the villages and are high on the tourist sights list. I believe this is gross. If tourists didn't go to gawk at and photograph them, these atrocities committed on women would die out.

But I gave in to an entreaty to visit the Jumping Cats Monastery; I would be drummed out of the Cat Lovers' Society if it got out that I had knocked this back. The Nga Hpe Kyaung Monastery is entirely made of teak and inside it was dark, wonderfully cool and inhabited, not only by a lot of cats, but some impressive ancient statues on ornate mosaic plinths. The cats that used to perform the jumping tricks have grown old now and are way past jumping. I know exactly how they feel. The monk who trained the cats died last year and there has been no one to teach new cats. But a lot of old pensioner cats lie about on a big straw mat and you can get down on the floor and play with them or use the small tea sets placed at intervals on the mat to have a cat tea party. The cats looked like the Blue Burmese breed but were much smaller. You would be too if, a natural carnivore, you were made to be a vegetarian. No meat can enter a Buddhist monastery.

After lunch at an over-the-water restaurant, I was taken to see the five hundred metre long teak footbridge that connects one village to the shore. When the water level drops in the dry season the people of this village are unable to use boats to go to the mainland so they built a marvellous bridge.

Every now and then we came upon a fisherman out on the lake using the style of rowing that is unique to Inle – standing in the back of the boat with a leg twined about an oar. This method evolved so that the rower could see over the weed that clogs the lake's shallow water. Mats of these weeds are used as a base for the floating gardens of the lake. We chugged slowly through them, passing along small lanes between rows of tomatoes and capsicum where egrets and ducks flew up as we disturbed them.

At four o'clock we returned to Nyaungshwe and I gave Kyaw ten thousand kyats, which judging by his smile must have been okay as a tip.

The date I needed be back in Yangon for my exit from Burma was approaching. I planned to catch the train to Thazi in Shwengang, the village on the main road near the turn off to Nyaungshwe. From Thazi, a whistle-stop on the Mandalay to Yangon train line, I could get a night train to Yangon. I had checked with the internet train guru, The Man in Seat

61, and had been assured that there were sleeper carriages on these trains.

The tuk tuk I had arranged to collect me arrived early the next morning and took me to the station. On the way I called into the Golden Kite restaurant. I had eaten dinner there the previous night and left my brolly hanging on the back of my chair. I am beginning to think I need a minder.

The ride back to the main road junction, me windblown in the little bouncing vehicle, seemed to last even longer than the one arriving in the taxi. But the nice driver dragged my bag over the rough ground of the yard and onto the station platform for me.

The ticket office was not open yet and I was told to wait until ten. At ten I was told, half an hour more. It was eleven before I was allowed to buy a ticket. Previously I had wondered why tickets were not sold before the train actually arrived. Now I know it is because there is a definite possibility that it may not come at all. They wait until they hear it is on the way.

The train was almost two hours late, but eventfully we left. As soon as we did it began to rain heavily into the open window beside my seat. A kind man came to help me close it when he saw me wrestling with it. This was when I remembered that I had left the retrieved brolley in the tuk tuk! The minder now becomes even more a reality.

We left the town and soon there were flame trees and yellow flowering trees like acacias beside the line. My seat was comfortable and I had plenty of room. Later the seats across from me were occupied by a woman and a cute little girl. A couple of women and a small boy sat in the seats on the opposite side of the aisle.

The train line is a marvel. It snakes along the very edge of high mountains, goes through deep cuttings and tunnels and crosses countless bridges. There was one massively impressive long, high viaduct. Approaching it, the train slowed almost to a stop, then proceeded toward it very cautiously at a walking pace. Once on the viaduct we were reduced to a crawl, literally inching along.

The scenery was sensational. In cuttings where creepers and vines grew into a dense green wall on both sides, tendrils reached out and brushed the sides of the train as we passed. At times leaves fell in on me and once I got smacked in the face by a small branch. In places enormous patches of rice were terraced down whole valleys ringed by jagged blue mountains. In other valleys large plots of vegetables grew. Sometimes I was looking down on verdant slopes from a great height where a motorbike on a far winding road was the size of an insect. There were patchworks of rice, corn and vegetables, some grown on bamboo trellises where the creepers of the vegetables formed a thick roof overhead. All was green and lush.

After four hours we arrived at Kalaw's pretty little railway station that looks like a Swiss chalet. Kalaw, originally another British hill station high in cool mountains, is a popular place from which to trek into the surrounding hills.

It took fifteen hours to reach Thazi, and we arrived three and a half hours late. We wouldn't have been so late if it had not been for the interminable stops the train made every few miles. The train ride had developed into a vegetable market. At each of the frequent stops a different vegetable specialty was on offer as well as food for the passengers. Once I was about to buy something in a small bag that looked interesting and edible but discovered that it was cut up carrots. Large amounts of vegetables were sold in commercial-sized bags and loads of them came aboard the train, and were stuffed in behind seats, in the aisle, wherever possible.

Time dragged on. The ride was wonderful but the stops became tedious and I could see no reason for them being so extended. We sat in Kalaw station for more than an hour and a half. It was half-past one in the morning when I finally climbed down from the train at Thazi. The station was a mess of people sleeping on straw mats or blankets on the cement platform floor under the tin roof. The passengers had had to dismount on the wrong side of the tracks and the rest of them nipped across the rails to the other side, but I could see the lights of an approaching train. I stood there feeling helpless. The tracks were deep and looked dangerous to cross in the dark. And my bag had to be carried.

Eventually a station person came to ask where I wanted to go. I said I wanted to take the sleeper train to Yangon the next night but right then I wanted a taxi to a guesthouse. Another man joined us, then another and still more until there were six men standing in a half circle around me all telling me the train to Yangon left at nine in the morning and that I should wait there until then as there was no taxi. 'No sleeper', they shouted like a Greek chorus. I knew this was rubbish and yet one of these men was the on-duty station master. Another man told me that he was the police – 'Special,' he said. Did that mean like the SS? He wore a faded T-shirt that said Ralph Lauren. I don't think so.

Finally they all escorted me across the tracks. The station master took me to a room next to his office and, unlocking a big padlock to let me in, said I could sleep there. Inside were two small, beat-up vinyl couches and several rows of the ubiquitous train station issue red plastic chairs. Ralph Lauren sat himself down in one, cross-legged with his bare feet pointed away from me, as is polite. The rest joined him. Were they going to watch me all night? It was unnerving. But eventually they got the message and left me to it.

I slept semi-concertinaed on a short couch for an hour and then got up to answer the insistent demand of my bladder. I asked the station master where the toilet was and he pointed out the back – the dark backyard of the station yard. I didn't find the loo out there but I did find a horse and cart and its driver sleeping on the seat. Great was my joy. 'Guesthouse?' I shouted to wake him. He nodded. I grabbed him and trotted him to my bag which he dutifully carried back to the cart.

Collecting the rest of my things, I departed as fast as I could, thanking the station master as I went. He didn't want me to go but nothing was going to keep me from a possible bed, not to mention a toilet.

Clip-clopping through the three-in-the-morning pitch dark around town, we came to the Wonderful Guesthouse. It was secured all across its front with heavy iron screens as though they were expecting the Mongol hordes to descend on them in the night. I had a horrible feeling it was closed for good. It looked abandoned. And there was only one other place to stay in this town. But the driver knew better. He located a bell and rang it insistently and repeatedly until a light came on. I stood there looking as pathetic as I could. Bedraggled and frowsy as I was, this wasn't hard. They were full, the woman said. I pleaded for a bed, looking even more forlorn. Then the kind woman said, 'You like the manager's room?' Would I ever!

As she let me in she said, 'I cannot charge you for this room. I just give you'. I insisted and forced half the usual rate of ten dollars on her. The room was tiny and really just a store room with a bed crammed in among shelves loaded with towels, sheets, blankets and cleaning supplies. But it had a toilet, oriental, but *stationary*. Something that has enormous appeal after train loos in Burma. There was also a hose fixture on the wall to act as a shower.

Gratefully, I fell on the bed. There were no sheets but a blanket was good enough. After a couple of hours I surfaced and the owner fed me egg and bread, coffee and banana. Then a thought occurred to me. 'Does the manager usually sleep in that room you gave me?' 'No, my son does'. This was the good-looking young man who helped to run the place, who was right then smiling at me. I was amazed he could still smile at me after I had turfed him out of his bed at three am. Wonderful indeed, was this place.

When I left I gave the rightful owner of the bed I had used the pillow I had bought for the night on the bus. It was filled with silicon and was not the usual cheap affair of the market. I had bought it in upmarket Ocean Supermarket and it had cost a whole four dollars.

Then I asked Madame if she knew about the possibility of getting a sleeper on the night train. She did. Madame knew much more than the station staff. She insisted on walking me 'five minutes' – twenty was more like it – to the station. Now the day-time station master was in charge and he knew all about sleepers. He and his two assistants set about phoning Mandalay. It took a lot of effort by these three smiling young men, but in the end they did produce a ticket for a sleeper on the six pm train to Yangon. It was a relief to know I would have a bed of my own that night.

I slept some more and surfaced to go down the street to a restaurant for lunch. It was a beer hall full of men who regarded me with extreme interest. I think I had missed the place Madame had directed me to.

At train time I took a horse cart, the local means of transport, to the station. It had poured rain for the last two hours and I had sat watching it and thinking about the brolly I had just lost. That little pink umbrella had been with me for years since I had bought it in Laos. It had learned to look after itself and must also have had a charmed life because I had left it behind in cafes, shops, markets, buses, hotels, anywhere I could in fact. People were forever running after me with it or I was trotting back to retrieve it. But, sadly, there was no going back for it this time. I hope the tuk tuk man would be kind to it.

The train arrived from Mandalay bang on time at six pm. Among the crowd on the platform I was the only foreigner, but I had three station workers looking after me, carrying my baggage and shepherding me along like a visiting film star. All that was missing was the red carpet. They saw me installed in my sleeping compartment of the one sleeper carriage on this long train. Then we all shook hands and they waved me off. It was going to be a shock to go home and be treated like a mere mortal after Burma.

The train quickly gathered speed and we lolloped along at a cracking pace, rocking and rolling and making a very satisfactory train-type sound. Soon we were in countryside that looked a bit dryish now and then. Later, as we went south, there were extensive areas of crops and rice and buffalos, cows and goats. An attendant wandered by with a menu. I ordered and food was produced shortly after. I had asked for noodles and chicken. I got a massive pile of fried rice. I left some on a station platform for one of those poor stray dogs. This train was different again from other sleepers I had had. However, none of them had been new in the last forty years. This compartment had only two berths with narrow beds one above the other and the usual open window. The metal sides were beat up, scratched and scuffed and covered with just plain dirt. A good scrub would have helped a lot. But in general it was superficially clean. At least there was a clean sheet on the cloth seat and a little pillow-cased cushion.

This was a real express train, unlike some that are called express but aren't. We only stopped for five minutes at a few stations and actually passed through others, something other trains seemed incapable of doing. I slept after a less than satisfactory visit to the heaving oriental loo. It was nice to sleep with my face level with an open window but it was strange to wake up when we had stopped in a station and find people on the platform closely inspecting me.

chapter 18

This journey was fast and in twelve and half hours I was in Yangon station. Five minutes before arrival people appeared on the train offering taxis. I accepted one man and he lumped my bag out onto the platform where he sold me to a driver, an older man who insisted on taking my hand to lead me down the stairs. At the bottom stood a posse of other hopeful drivers, who cheered and clapped my guardian as though he had secured the prize. Which he had. He charged me double the going rate. We got into his old car and lumbered off. No sitting in the back with this bloke driving, he almost pushed me into the front seat with him.

Early morning Yangon was alive with street vendors and monks making their alms rounds. Motherland welcomed me back and had me in my room, after the compulsory breakfast, by eight o'clock.

Three hours' sleep later I staggered out to wash. The water from my new room's sink flowed down over my feet to exit via a convenient hole in the floor. Easier than mending the break in the pipe, but where else would you have to strip to your knickers to wash your hands?

Treating the sandfly bites I had received that morning from the resident population that live in the trees outside Motherland, I discovered a great scratch five inches long on the back of my arm. I rushed to look at the shirt I had just discarded, realising that a cut like this had to have been made on a bare arm. It was. The shirt had a large three-cornered tear down the sleeve. This must have happened when I fell over. Do not read on if you are eating – I fell over in the toilet on the train. A pongy, wet, squat toilet. The train had been shaking from side to side like a dog with a rat when a sudden more violent lurch rocked me over sideways, and down I went, bashing the side wall with my arm. I had hung on to a pipe, desperate not to descend totally to the mess on the floor. When the train straightened, I clawed myself upright. Thankfully I had managed to keep my clothes off the floor. I filled the plastic dipper from the tap that was used for flushing – you didn't expect a push-button toilet here, did you? – to wash my feet and shoes. Fortunately this toilet was not in the appalling condition that some were, but I disinfected my cut anyway.

It had rained heavily during the morning and now it was damp and muggy, humid and grey. I borrowed a brolly from the receptionist and walked to the Ocean supermarket to buy a replacement for my lost one. Now I have Pink Umbrella Mark 10 or something near that number. Due to an ingrained superstition that it is bad luck to open an umbrella inside, I did not know until I opened my previous umbrella outside the shop that it sported a big picture of Snoopy dog, which I then had to live with for years. Opening the latest one in the street, I discovered that it had a picture of Barbie, as well as 'My favourite doll' written on it. At least I like Snoopy. I loathe stick-insect Barbie.

Happily ensconced at Motherland, I slept for another ten hours. At breakfast the next morning the waiter said to me, 'You always smiling'. I replied, 'I am always happy to be here'. Why not, it was true. I had finally learned to say, *yesu ting ba be* (thank you) and it was received with delight.

I took a taxi to see the glass factory I had seen on a TV programme in Australia. It was a long way, at first on a highway, then on an unmarked dirt road that turned into a tiny rutted lane where thick jungle crowded the car each side. Finally we arrived at a wreck of a place. The factory had closed. Behind it in an old open-sided shed, a jumble of heavily dust-covered glassware cluttered a couple of large wooden tables. What remained of the stock was pretty ordinary looking stuff, but apparently in the past this small factory had produced some very fine glass.

An elderly gentleman told me that the TV programme had been done several years ago and that they had had to close because natural gas for the kiln had gone up to thirty times its original price. He said that glass makers from the famous Italian Murano company as well as from Australia had called there when they were operating. He showed me samples of the sand and potash he had used in his process. The sand certainly was very fine and white. I bought two pieces, more as an act of charity than because they were any good. They are both pale green, a frog and a paperweight.

By the time I left him the taxi driver and I had spent two hours together. Unusually for Burma he had a fair command of English and we had some conversation. He asked me if Burma was known in Australia. Tentatively I said that Aung San Suu Kyi was known. Not so long ago merely speaking her name got you a gaol sentence (she was referred to only as The Lady), and I was still cautious about saying it. But he beamed and showed me her photo on his phone.

He dropped me at the market where I bought a painting from the crippled boy who is always there, haunting the entrance. He hobbles along on crutches and seems to have a displaced hip; one leg is withered and hangs loosely at an angle. I had fobbed him off on all my previous visits but this would be my last. Then I ate lunch in a market cafe where I gave a donation to a pink-robed Buddhist nun in return for a blessing after watching her be rudely dismissed by two horrible Europeans. Later I passed a tiny, very old nun, and, seeing that her small begging bowl was empty, I chased after her and dropped a couple of notes in it. As I did, I looked up to see a stallholder smiling at me. People sometimes did this when I gave to beggars too, so I think it was okay.

I walked across the road to where I had been told there is another market, but didn't find it. I went in an ornate gate that I thought could be its entrance, but was met by a man who indicated that I should have my shoes off as I was actually entering a mosque. I backed out and walked on, thinking I was heading towards the Queens Park Hotel, but when the Sule Pagoda appeared at the end of the road I knew I wasn't. I ended up on the waterfront, having gone in the completely opposite direction. Why do I keep trying? Perhaps because on the rare occasion that I get it right it gives me such a thrill.

This day was Saturday and downtown Yangon's streets were packed with people. There were countless small street stalls and one lane I went up had second-hand electrical bits and pieces strewn on the ground. Another wide street's broken and lumpy but tree-shaded footpaths were covered with groups of men sitting on low stools clustered around small boxes commandeered as tea tables. On them sat pots of tea and small handle-less cups like saki cups. This seemed to be some sort of club. Then someone asked me, 'You want stones?', and I realised that they were discussing, and probably dealing in, jade or other gems. I saw only a little produced; maybe that came later when the tea drinking was over. These groups continued for miles.

As I walked I watched the sky become darker and darker and a huge inky cloud gathering, approaching from the sea. Time to give up walking. I hailed a taxi and rode back to Motherland with a driver who told me that he was from South India where people who had been to Australia to work in films had told him about our cheese and milk products. This was what I missed most from home – cheese. Order cheese on something here and you got those appallingly uncheese-like plastic-wrapped slices. And at about a dollar a slice.

It started to rain as I left the taxi at Motherland, and it was dark and thundering so I decided I was finished for the day. As this was my last day I used all my remaining phone credit to call home and check on the cat. The cat said she was fine. The phone credit had lasted all the time I was in Burma, pretty good for a twenty-three dollar card – twenty-eight days of local and one international phone call.

At dinner I made the fatal mistake of thinking it was a good idea to try something Western on the menu before I left. It was not. I ordered 'Maxican burger'. Maxican, whatever that was, it might have been, but burger it certainly wasn't. It came with an enormous pile of skinny chips that I gave to a young English couple sitting nearby who told me that they had been teaching in South Korea.

At breakfast I donated all my tatty, indescribably worn, torn and dirty small kyat notes to the kitchen staff. It made an impressively large wad but probably was no more than a couple of dollars. No one minds the state of the local money but they refuse to take a US dollar that is not in pristine condition.

Sadly I had to leave Burma, and took a taxi through the heavy Sunday traffic to the airport. Remembering that I needed to get rid of my remaining kyats – it is illegal to export them, and why would you when all they would be good for outside Burma would be to wallpaper the loo – I scouted around for something to spend them on and opted for a four thousand kyat bottle of Mandalay rum, strictly as a souvenir of course.

In the departure lounge I observed the local attitude to litter. A plastic bag lay on the carpet. Two stewardesses stepped over it, one kicked it to the side. Other airport employees did the same. It occurred to no one to put it in the bin, even though, for a change, there was actually a bin in sight – the only one I had seen in this area. I itched to pick up the bag before someone tripped on it – it had already entangled a few feet – but I was curious to see what happened. It was still there when I boarded the plane.

I arrived in Bangkok towards evening and with difficulty found a taxi. The driver shouted information at me for the entire hour it took to get downtown, only one word of which I understood – 'Bangkok'. In the central area of the town long avenues of trees were hung with masses of golden fairy lights that were just then coming on, making for a pretty sight in the grey cloud of approaching rain. Then, passing a big picture of Queen Sirikit, the driver shouted, 'Clean'. I'm sure she is, but the other word he used escaped me. More pictures followed and I realised that it was her *birthday* and what he was saying was not 'Clean birdie' but 'Queen birthday'. He added then that she was 'one hundled an tenty.' She would be thrilled. Probably have had him beheaded in the old days. I know she's even older than I am, but 120! I don't think so. I said, 'Queen Sirikit and King Bhumipol' and impressed him no end. I am always surprised at how much the Thais love their royal family. Then there were pictures of the crown prince. I rather hoped my driver would tell me he was the Clown Plince but he didn't.

At Kho San Street the evening was thick with drunken louts of tourists. Moving into my room at the Palace, I decided to try a wee sip of my four dollar bottle of rum. But when I opened it, I discovered that it was not intended for keeping. The lid did not screw back on. You were meant to get it all down in one go. Of course I couldn't waste it, so life was a little hazy from then on.

A day later I boarded the train to the south, very glad to leave Bangkok, especially Kao San Street – the tourists there were mostly an embarrassment. I had bought a train ticket to Hat Yai before I had left for Burma, planning to travel from there across to Songhla the 'city between two seas', an ancient trading port situated in the narrowest part of the Thai peninsular between the Gulf of Thailand and the Andaman Sea. I intended to stay there until it was time to go to Singapore and catch the *Buxstar* home.

I looked up Songhla on the internet and to my horror found a big red warning from Smart Traveller, the Australian government travel advisory website. It was the fourth and final stage of their warnings. One is, take usual precautions, two, travel with extreme care, three, travel only if necessary and four – in letters of fire – DO NOT TRAVEL. I checked other sites. They were all the same. And they included Hat Yai. This area that straddles the Thai/ Malaysian border was formerly an Islamic kingdom called Pattani and this is where the majority of Thailand's largest religious minority group, Muslims, live. Some of them want an independent state and opt for secession. A radical few want to use insurrection and armed resistance to obtain it. This has led to terrorism, and frequent bombings and shootings occur. A policeman was killed two days after I crossed the border there.

Oh, poo. My ticket to Hat Yai was paid, so I had to go. But Songhla, the city between two seas, would have to wait. I decided that when I reached Hat Yai I would keep moving south to Penang Island in Malaysia. This seemed a nice safe place to spend the ten days I had to wait before going down to Singapore.

My two-berth sleeping compartment on the train was excellent. On arrival at Hat Yai at nine in the morning, only two hours late, a young man took possession of me on the station platform. When I said, 'Penang', he said, 'Mini bus', and trundled my bag out of the yard, across the road and down the street to an office where I paid twenty dollars to get all the way to the island. There was no need now to go to Butterworth and take a ferry across, like in the old days. Since 1985 there has been a wonderful enormously long bridge.

chapter **19**

The five-hour trip was comfortable. I was ferried across town to the mini bus in a lovingly polished, elderly yellow Mercedes driven by an old fellow who clutched the wheel tightly with two fists and drove very slowly, peering through the windscreen intently like a learner. The two immigration posts at the Thai/Malaysian border were painless, but I am extremely careful still at borders after the trouble I'd had previously. I would have been even more cautious if I had known that a policeman would be killed there two days later.

By five in the afternoon we were at Georgetown, the capital of Penang Island. The bridge crossing had been a breeze and I marvelled at the engineering feat that had created it – a thirteen and a half kilometre wonder. In Georgetown the bus trip finished in the centre of town at Komtar, the transport hub, where I found a taxi driver and asked him to take me to a hotel on the beach.

He turned out to be another chatty fellow but this time I could understand him. He said he would take me to the less expensive and less touristed beach. He did, and at the Naza Taiyya Hotel at Tanjong Tokong I negotiated a price for a room for a week.

The hotel had an absolute beachfront position and the sea views from my room on the fifth floor were spectacular. It overlooked a long sweep of sandy coast, lined with coconut palms and mangrove trees, that curved around to a far headland. Directly in front, the hotel was a little island covered with green trees that looked close enough for me to swim out to, and on one side was the misty outline of Sumatra. Along the beach beside the hotel was the Chinese Swimming Club and I could look down from my room into their Olympic-sized pool and watch swimmers training in the lanes. Behind that the distant skyline was pierced now and then by thirty- or forty-storeyed narrow blocks of buildings. They were unattractive to my eye, and I wondered why they didn't topple over.

At night I would leave the sliding door to my room's balcony open so that I could hear the surf breaking on the sand below and see the rain, which came most nights, accompanied by flashes of sheet lightning that lit up the entire sky.

Next morning I managed to catch a bus to the centre. The receptionist told me that the bus that stopped on the hotel's side of the road went to the city but that the bus on the opposite side of the road went to the beach at Batu Ferringhi. But I was so sure I had come up the other side of the road from town in the taxi, I stood there instead.

I waited at the stop with a gathering crowd for thirty-five minutes watching six buses go by until finally one pulled over and let us on. And, I went to the beach! Enough said. It took a long time to come back again but I had plenty to spare, so why not?

I began my way to town again and eventually arrived at Komtar, the transport centre from where I had started the day before. Close by I caught the free 'hop on and off' tourist bus, seemingly patronised almost entirely by locals; tourists who did arrive were swamped in the stampede to get on. After a while I began to be able to work out where I was. The bus passed some lovely buildings. The central area of Georgetown has been proclaimed 'World Heritage' and there were marvellous sights everywhere I looked. The bus also stopped at the impressive *Queen Elizabeth II* pier from where the ferry runs to Butterworth on the Malaysian mainland.

Penang was established as a British trading post in 1786

and became part of the federated states of Malaysia in 1957. Although Malaysians are mostly Muslim, Georgetown is a mixed bag of ethnicity and religions. Chinese, Indian and other Asian cultures all seem to cohabit with tolerance. I saw every possible style of dress in the streets and within a few feet of each other there were Christian churches – Methodist, Anglican, Adventist and Catholic – and Buddhist and Hindu temples as well as many mosques.

Back at the end of the tourist bus circuit I went into a nearby shopping plaza. Many of these temples to the God Mammon dot the landscape of Penang. Shopping seemed to be the national sport. In this mall I found brilliant shops full of feminine gee gaws, thousands of pieces of jewellery and ornaments, all very cheap but pretty. Many were for use on head coverings or as hair decorations. Make something taboo and this is what happens. It becomes a focus of attention.

None of my three adaptors fitted the electric plugs here so the next day I walked to Tesco's, two bus stops towards the city, where I was assured I would find one. Wow, what an enormous supermarket, with an incredible range of goods – some of the assistants zoomed about the place on roller skates. But the extensive meat and fish counters left a lot for the hygiene police to focus their attentions on. They were all open to the air, not to mention fingers. And smelly too. Even though the goods were packed in ice I didn't fancy this method of display. The bakery goods were on open trays too and I saw a small boy poking the cakes. Nice. I bought cheese and a local hard crunchy chip, which, I found later turned out to be a mistake.

Returning to the Naza, I decided to investigate a side road. Well, truthfully, I thought it would be a short cut along the beach but I am becoming increasingly embarrassed about admitting the mistakes I make. This small road, lined both sides by rows of tiny, two-storied wooden houses fronted by plants in big pots, led to a lovely little bay piled with huge rocks on which the sea broke in spray. On one side was a large old red- and gold-painted Chinese temple, and on the other, high on a cliff above the water, was a ramshackle cafe. There was a stone breakwater with a couple of small boats moored at it, but there was no further access along the coast. This bay was enclosed.

Back in my room after this detour, I munched on the rock-hard crisps and broke a tooth – a front incisor. I had a seriously horrible-looking gap where a piece of tooth had gone missing. I must have swallowed it! I needed a dentist, fast. The reception desk people gave me the name of a *doctor gigi* ('*gigi*' is the wonderful Malay word for teeth) not far away. I checked the clinic out on Trip Advisor on the internet and decided to risk it. In the past I had read conflicting reports from health tourists who had come to Malaysia for what would have been far more expensive treatments in their home countries. Some told horror stories, others were all praise.

I took the bus four stops in the town direction to the surgery where I was shown immediately into the dentist's chair. And I was out and fixed in twenty minutes! I had imagined injections, several visits and long consultations about treatment and cost. But a slim young woman of few words sat me down, opened my mouth and set to work. No discussion, no waffle. She and her two assistants belted into me like mechanics doing a tyre change at a pit stop in a car race. There was just drilling and pasting and, most of all, there was no pain. My tooth looked great, better than before, a perfect match for the one on the other side – and it cost a mere thirty six dollars.

I spent ten days exploring Georgetown. There were many places to eat and the food was very good, super cheap and available everywhere despite it being Ramadan, the Muslim month of fasting. In Chinatown once I passed a tiny two-storeyed shop house, only a few feet wide, with a balcony upstairs. A large sign on it said, 'The Great Wall Waving Parlour', which I think may have meant that it was a hairdressing establishment. But my warped sense of humour immediately had a vision of people paying their two ringgit and being allowed to climb the stairs to stand on the small balcony overlooking the street and do a QEII royal wave act.

The first time I took the bus back from the town I missed my stop and ended up at Batu Ferringhi beach again. But the ride there was exceedingly pretty, with lots of coves and cliffs and little beaches and bays to see. Buses were a good way to meet local people. At bus stops they always smiled and said hello and chatted if they could, unlike most Europeans I came across, who generally studiously avoided looking at strangers.

The national museum was interesting. Being fond of old cars, I especially liked their vintage Rolls Royce, despite the thirty-five bullet holes in its chassis. In 1951 communist guerrillas assassinated Sir Henry Gurney, the British high commissioner, in this car. Beside it was a Scammel Hornet, a peculiar-looking large three-wheeled truck that had once been used as a work horse all over the island.

After a while I began to understand the writing on signs and a little of what people said so I started using my rusty Indonesian. It came in handy in Lorong Kulit, the thieves market, where it helped with bargaining and at least made it *look* like I had some local knowledge.

In the evenings when it was cooler I liked to walk along the beach. Wreckage from the 2004 tsunami still remained in front of the Chinese Swimming Club. A pair of big iron gates, still padlocked but twisted at an awkward angle, lay rusting on the sand, along with a huge tree tipped sideways but still in a massive concrete pot. It was hard to imagine water could do that.

Every morning after breakfast I would sit in the hotel foyer and read the local English language newspaper, some articles in which changed my view that Malaysia had a liberal Islamic legal system. One day the court news reported that a young woman had been imprisoned because she had posted Ramadan good wishes with a photo of herself and her two dogs on Facebook. (The dogs were a No No.) And a man was sent to gaol for six years and given a beating with the rattan for stealing a hat and a mobile phone. Another man was sentenced to death by hanging for murder but at the same time was given eight years gaol for assault. I wondered how that would be worked out.

I had forgotten that the holiday at the end of Ramadan was approaching, so I received a rude shock when I tried to book my room for another three days and was told that the hotel was full. Five hours on the internet later I had still not found another hotel room. Even hostels were fully booked. I had the same problem with getting a seat on a bus to Singapore, and had to buy a ticket for one that went only as far as Johor Bahru on the Malaysian side of the Strait. This was not a problem. It is not far from JB to Singapore and I would be able get there easily with a share taxi, but it was another of the dreaded night buses.

Fortunately I was saved from sleeping on the street. The hotel manager received a cancellation and told me I could keep my room. Then it was the holiday celebration of Ide el Fittr (the feast of the lazy mechanic). There were fireworks at night and crowds of people staying in the hotel, including some Saudis, the women in full purdah. I watched them load their plates from the special sumptuous array on the breakfast buffet and wondered how they were going to eat it in public while wearing a total face veil. It took me back to my days in Saudi with a shock. I had forgotten how restricting of all normal interaction it is for women to have their faces obscured. One small woman trotted back and forth with plates for her large husband who was seated close to me, but I did not see her eat.

My last day came. The bus left Komtar at nine pm, but then spent two hours messing around before it finally left the island. Driving over the long bridge to the mainland, the dark night pretty with lights twinkling on surrounding boats and along the waterfront, we reached the four-lane main highway south along the peninsula and joined a traffic jam. Packed solid in a horde of vehicles, we crawled along for hours. This was the post-holiday crowd returning home from Ide celebrations.

We arrived at Johor Bahru bus station at eleven the next morning, six hours late, and I lined up with a mob of people to wait my turn for a share taxi to Singapore. Immigration and customs were simple procedures and I was soon across the causeway and deposited at the hotel I had booked in Singapore, the Fragrance Emerald in Geylang. I was in the red light district again.

The Buxstar's Singapore agent sent me a message with the ship's arrival time and said that their driver would collect me at six the next evening. With a day to fill, I took a bus to Bugis Street and, walking around, came across the Singapore library. A fabulous place, I spent a happy afternoon there and, looking up my name in their catalogue, was pleased to find four of my books listed with photos of their covers.

That evening, collected and delivered to the wharf, I was welcomed onto the *Buxstar* again. The captain, who was going on leave, was handing the ship over to a new master, a youngish Ukrainian man. There was only one other passenger, a male New Zealander. There was also a new cook, another Filipino who proved to be an excellent cook, and the food improved considerably. There were other new faces too, all Filipino, but sadly I found that Handsome Harry, the second officer with the fabulous smile, had signed off. Singapore is the *Buxstar*'s home port so this is where contracts begin and end.

This time I had a cabin much the same as my previous one but on the fifth deck. (One hundred and twenty more steps per day to get fed and watered, but who was counting.)

The ship spent all that day and until eight the next morning at the wharf, loading containers. The harbour was crowded with countless vessels. From the deck or my porthole I watched a constant movement of them coming and going.

Apart from freighters – the *Irina*, *Hamburg Sud*, CMA, CGM, *Hanjin* – there were the blue-and-white fast-cruiser police boats, battered old junks, and the always busily coming-and-going pilots and tugs.

We left port and, passing a small lump of an island covered with green trees that divided the waters at the entrance to the harbour, sailed out onto a calm grey sea. Towards nightfall thirty-six hours later, we approached Jakarta. As we drew near the wharf a small boat without lights circled us in the darkness. 'They are not pirates, only robbers,' I was reassured by a deckhand, who added that all the access points on our ship had been already secured with boarding repellers. Jakarta is not a safe port. Work began as soon as we tied up but, as the ship was due to leave early the next morning, no shore leave was posted.

I stood on the deck as we left port and sailed slowly along a curved breakwater with a red lighthouse on the end of it. On the other side of the breakwater were dozens of water craft, from a fisherman in a rowboat to big freighters. As we sailed south toward the north-west coast of Australia, two warm, pleasant days and lovely cool tropical nights followed, and it was delightful to be out on deck.

At breakfast the following morning the second officer told me that our ship had been diverted to the locality of a sinking boat that had sent an SOS. We were not in busy shipping lanes here and the *Buxstar* was the only ship in the area apart from the Australian navy ship *Parramatta*, which was also on its way. We had been told to rescue the two hundred refugees on board the ship. I queried how we could find room for that many people and was told that this was not a consideration. It was necessary and it would be done.

I changed into suitable working gear in case there were casualties and went up to the bridge to watch proceedings. The atmosphere was tense. I stood in a corner looking out over the wide expanse of lonely dark blue sea, empty except for a few white caps, listening to calls from the Australian search and rescue plane and the HMAS *Parramatta*. Eight of the crew scanned the sea intently, five with binoculars. It came to me then that the drills we had done were for real. That wide empty sea that looks so benign is also deadly.

Suddenly a seaman shouted. 'Small craft on the starboard side!' We slowed, but it was a fishing vessel. In time we neared the area of the distress call and received a chilling message from the plane – 'No ship sighted, search now for survivors'. The ship had sunk! I was shocked. It had not occurred to me that we might be too late. Another message came that life rafts had been sighted and the *Parramatta* was now coming to collect them. We were told to continue looking for survivors and we did so until the aircraft told us we were released from the search and rescue effort and could return to our course.

The captain told me later that it had been 14 degrees in the water and that the ship had gone down about the time the call came, five hours before help arrived – too long to stay alive at that temperature, he said. He looked upset. Some people had most likely died. Maybe he blamed himself for not getting there sooner.

It took many hours to get back to our correct position, but there was no word of complaint from the crew. One day another ship might have to come to their rescue. This is the unwritten law of the sea. I had wondered why so many crew had been needed to look for as big an item as a ship but now I realised that they had known what I did not – that a ship that had begun to sink hours beforehand had very likely sunk by then. What they had been searching for so diligently were people in the water. In Australia later I heard news reports that said five people were known to have drowned when this ship sank but that possibly there had been more.

Four days later we reached Fremantle. There was a long shore leave here and I was able to spend all day and evening catching up with old friends. It was a beautiful sunny day and as I walked around the streets of the port waiting to be collected I was impressed with how much Fremantle had gone ahead in the years since I had lived in Perth and worked at the Fremantle hospital. I was driven up to Perth along the well-remembered road I used to travel every day, happy to see familiar sites. We had a lovely time and I did not return back on board until late that night.

Then the *Buxstar* sailed out into the Great Australian Bight and I was on my way home again.

Wakefield Press is an independent publishing and distribution company based in Adelaide, South Australia.
We love good stories and publish beautiful books.
To see our full range of books, please visit our website at
www.wakefieldpress.com.au
where all titles are available for purchase.

Find us!

Twitter: www.twitter.com/wakefieldpress
Facebook: www.facebook.com/wakefield.press
Instagram: instagram.com/wakefieldpress